MINSTER PUBLISHING

Paul Williams divides hi   n old
chocolate factory just yard   stone
olive mill with an Arab l   áláaga.
In rare moments of repos   ster at
Winchester College where he taught languages for many years. He has
been happily married since 1971.

The author, 1969.

i

THE BANKER

WHO TURNED TO VOODOO

Paul Williams

Published by Pen Press in association with Minster Publishing
www.thebankerwhoturnedtovoodoo.com

Copyright © Paul Williams 2011

Paul Williams asserts the moral right to
be identified as the author of this work

Cover design © PFA Williams

ISBN 978-1-78003-331-0

For
Melissa, Edmund and Patrick

I thus learnt my first great lesson in the inquiry into these obscure fields of knowledge, never to accept the disbelief of great men or their accusations of imposture or of imbecility, as of any weight when opposed to the repeated observation of facts by other men, admittedly sane and honest. The whole history of science shows us that whenever the educated and scientific men of any age have denied the facts of other investigators on *a priori* grounds of absurdity or impossibility, the deniers have always been wrong.

Alfred Wallace: *Notes on the Growth of Opinion as to Obscure Psychical Phenomena During the Last Fifty Years*, 1893

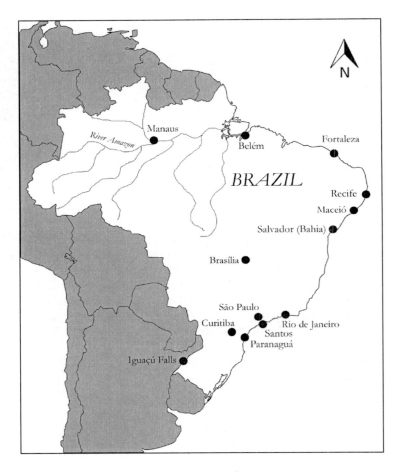

Map 1: Brazil

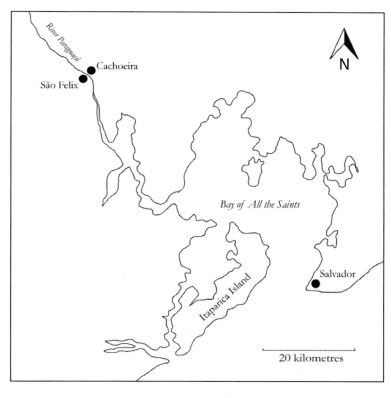

Map 2: Salvador and Bay of All the Saints

Contents

	Foreword	xiii
1	Tossing for it	1
2	London	5
3	Brazil	19
4	Salvador	23
5	Curitiba	53
6	Fortaleza	71
7	South to Rio	83
8	Rio de Janeiro	87
9	England	101
10	Goodbye to Banking	105
11	Douglas	107
12	St. Andrews	111
13	Partula	119
14	Brazil again	133
15	Some gods	137
16	Dona Cécé	151
17	Itaparica	155
18	A god and a devil	163
19	Dona Alice	169
20	Gnawing hunger	175
21	Cult of the dead	183
22	Raimunda	189
23	Spiritism	193

24	Cachoeira	199
25	Dona Isaura	221
26	Carmen	225
27	Vicente	233
28	A doctor, a teacher and a lawyer	243
29	God is Brazilian	251
30	Brazil's living dead	255

Foreword

Late 1968: the eve of my departure to Brazil. My father pored over an atlas.

'Where's this Brazil place you're going to?'

He had heard of Pele, Rio de Janeiro and the Sugar Loaf Mountain but probably thought, along with everybody else, that Carmen Miranda sang in Spanish and that Carnival only happened in Venice. Forty years on, outgoing President Lula is already a household name, Club Med devotees have heard of holiday destinations like Itaparica, and you don't have to be a football fanatic to know where *Maracaná* is.

When I went I felt like a pioneer. There was one reasonably reliable tourist guide, a slim tome that fitted easily into my suitcase, *The South American Handbook (1964 edition)* which, despite its title, covered Mexico and the Caribbean and all the countries of Central as well as South America. The editor mentions one of his regular contributors in an editorial: '...the wonder man who is sweating his way on a bicycle through Latin America...with fabulous zigzags into the interior. Now there's a young woman crossing the seas to marry him and soon two starry-eyed romantics will be pedalling, pedalling (a tandem?) north...and on to goodness knows where. And may all the bandits doff their sombreros as they go by'. Naturally I found this passage, with its hints of new discoveries and danger, extremely enticing but knew that my ever-anxious parents would not, so resolved never to show it to them. The *Handbook* went on to devote merely 115 pages to the largest of all the countries, Brazil, (of which 29 were full page black and white advertisements). Rio de Janeiro, the city with most international fame, was allocated no more than 14 full pages. The section 'How to reach Brazil' started by devoting half a page to 'steamship services', then only five lines to 'air services', stating proudly: 'The air journey from London to Rio takes *only* 14 hours 55 minutes' (my italics).

Bureaucracy, as in most developing countries, was rife and infuriating but it had its funny side. Full-sized posters in Post Offices said that all envelopes should bear on the reverse the name and address of the sender and any letter not complying would be returned to the sender. Post office officials were blind to the madness of this edict. Envelopes did not come with a convenient strip of glue on the flap, nor did stamps, so unwieldy pots of glue stuck (literally) on shelves near the Post Office counter generated long queues. Men with plastic briefcases bulging with their clients' income tax documents, gas, electricity and rates bills, identity card and passport applications stood patiently in lines in all Government offices. You paid them a pittance to do all the waiting while you got on with your job.

Residence permits demanded that you personally should spend a long morning in a queue waiting to have black ink pasted on all ten fingers which were then roughly pressed by a uniformed civil servant on the ten blank squares printed on the application form. Then there was a two-minute peremptory medical consisting of a stab with a stethoscope and a glance into one eye, and this resulted in a magnificent official document covered in impressive stamps certifying that the bearer was not suffering from 'leprosy, T.B., elephantiasis, trachoma, V.D., cancer, mental disturbance'. Nor was he 'blind, deaf, deaf-and-dumb, wounded, mutilated, an alcoholic or a drug addict', nor did he have any 'organic lesion' preventing him from working. Across the top was a red rubber stamp declaring: 'The revolution of 1964 is irrevocable. It will consolidate democracy in Brazil'.

For the first two weeks of your stay certain aspects of the bureaucracy got you down, but some of the madness was cheering: a brand new glass and steel hotel had lavatories with see-through glass doors and no locks. The official management line was that you didn't need locks if you could see the lavatory was occupied. The orange plastic net used for packaging citrus fruit was always carefully opened by street urchins then worn on the head (not torn and then discarded as in Britain). Coca Cola was tipped down blocked lavatories to ease the blockage (and it worked too). I once paid a 15p bus fare with no fewer than 47 *Cruzeiro* notes that were all legal currency at the time. Communications were poor: telephones hardly connected one city to another and businesses relied on telex machines, hence the abundance of ticker tape showers from top floors every time the national side won a football match.

Now that Brazil is on the brink of economic success and about to join ranks with the world's leading industrial nations this book's title may at first sight seem out of place, yet another story from Latin America rooted in the unbelievable in the style of García Márquez or Isabel Allende. But it's really a true story, a memoir and a travel book covering the two years I spent as a well-paid banker in different parts of Brazil, followed by a third year when I struggled as a research student with no grant and a virtually non-existent income. *The Banker Who Turned To Voodoo* tells my story and recaptures the flavour of what life was like in the late 1960s when there was still a very small middle class and all wealth was controlled by an even smaller, obscenely rich minority. In 1968 the population was under 90 million; today (2011) it is over 190 million. In the intervening period towns and cities have been transformed in order to accommodate this huge increase and the ensuing social upheaval has been marked. One of my purposes behind writing the book is to record what life was like a comparatively short while ago when no-one in government, or indeed elsewhere, was predicting what has now come about: Brazil, one of the great economic success stories of modern times.

In the late 60s the desperately poor who made up the vast majority of the population clamoured for food and yet proudly followed the huge and ambitious projects successive governments embarked on. Now, they have finally been given real and tangible hope. The incoming President, wishing to follow in Lula's footsteps, has declared that she will 'eradicate poverty'.

Neither I nor anyone else thought that was remotely realistic forty years ago when a large part of the population was still to a greater or lesser extent caught up in ancient practices handed down by the slaves, when busy road junctions in cities from São Paulo to Manaus were littered with offerings to the gods, and the throb of drums could be heard late at night in the outer suburbs of cities. Brazil's African culture seemed to drive an invisible stake between the modernisers embarking on sumptuous projects financed with seemingly limitless foreign money, and the ordinary people struggling to survive on or near the bread line while remaining happily convinced that their rich fully-integrated African heritage along with other national treasures such as the ever-successful football team and hundreds of miles of glistening beaches were unequalled in the world. Surprisingly, the ancient practices have survived and are now more flourishing than ever before. The gullible young man who first worked as a Bank trainee then as a student in Brazil in the 1960s was well aware of them affecting the lives of the men and women he came across at the time. He has now gone on to plot the astonishing progress of African-based ritual in the midst of the new, vibrant society that Brazil has since become.

1

Tossing for it

The coin spun up towards the nicotine-stained ceiling of the saloon bar catching some of the light from the windows then remained suspended for a brief second in mid air. Ridiculous as it may sound, the course of the next few years of my life resided in that coin and everything depended on how it would fall.

I had been offered two possible jobs in my last term at Cambridge: a temporary ministerial post in the Honduras government, Tegucigalpa, Central America, (the address sounded perfect), with special responsibility for increasing the English market for Honduran bananas (this bit sounds unbelievable, I know), fluent Spanish essential, accommodation and subsistence expenses included, but no pay because in those days volunteers for developing countries were expected to subsist on nothing. I liked the romance of experiencing poverty and felt flattered by a Cabinet post which, so I naively assumed, could lead on to permanent influential positions in high places. I might have an opposite number in London who could put in a word for me. Just the ticket. I didn't give a moment's thought to the fact that it couldn't have been a proper Cabinet post so I wouldn't have a vote. Cabinet probably meant small desk in large room with other small desks and lots of other small people, but if this thought crossed my mind it didn't stay there long. Nor did I imagine for a second that my opposite number would probably be just like me, setting out after University with one unsteady foot on the first rung, and absolutely no sway among his superiors until he'd put quite a few years behind him. But this job made me think more highly of myself than perhaps I should, and seemed to thrust me into a good position in an exotic land, so the very thought of it excited me.

The other job was safer, longer lasting, well paid and might send me to Brazil where I would pick up Portuguese. Again, I naively assumed that a degree in Spanish and French with a bit of self-taught Portuguese tacked on for good measure would create a springboard for higher things. But could I really stomach the idea of working for a Bank? I had a vivid memory of a florid little man whose head barely reached above the solid mahogany counter, wielding a tiny key and opening my book-shaped leather-bound brass savings box with National Provincial Bank embossed in gold on the cover. Navy blue for me; red for my sister. Would I become like him, be-suited, be-spectacled, unctuous guardian of other people's money, slowly dying of respectability, a sluggard in expectation of a safe pension? My instincts were firmly against it but parental and avuncular pressures were brought to bear at a time when a young man about to set off on life's journey pretended to listen for politeness' sake, although in fact he wasn't listening at all.

They were surprised and not a little disappointed when, fortified by a mouthful of the House best bitter and the whole sixties ethos of doing my own thing, I declared to all within earshot that I would toss for it and abide by the coin's decision. I had a half crown on me and lost no momentum. On striking the carpet it rolled under a table and became embroiled in chair legs so for a moment I was able to contemplate my future at floor level away from the general gaze. Damn. My heart was in Honduras but the coin shouted Bank, Bank, Bank. Older generations, overcome by a general sense of relief, applauded. The gov'nor stood me a drink.

Later I lay in my bed hearing the hours strike on the church clock on the hill, trying to convince myself that I could make a go of this but knowing deep down that the squareness of the peg and the roundness of the hole were already defining incompatibilities which in time would be clear for all to see. All I knew about banking (not much at this stage), filled me with considerable apprehension. I was no good at Maths for a start. I could manage adding up and subtraction but surely banking required advanced mathematical skills? The imminent trainee course which I was dreading would doubtless steer me through book-keeping and balance sheet analysis, but I'd spent the last few years analysing poetry which I considered a much more noble pursuit. Where on earth could they meet? I took just a small grain of comfort from Wodehouse's Psmith, a character I'd always admired, who didn't take kindly to banking in the City, although to be fair he wasn't too fond of the idea of work in the first place.

In a few weeks I would be donning a three piece suit and stiff collar and commuting from the heart of Surrey to the City, to all intents and purposes a City gent in the making, copy of today's *Times* under the left arm, leaving the right arm free to swing a perfectly rolled umbrella. Was this me? Well, some of it was. I'd always envied people who dressed up and paced the boards (Psmith) and that, in a way, was precisely what I would be doing: going out on stage and acting a rôle for a few years until I'd had enough. I felt a fraudster before I started but as my elders said, I had nothing to lose. Well, they didn't have to do it, did they?

2

London

The Bank course for new trainees was predictably dull from day one though we were regularly assured by our instructors that things would get much more exciting in three months' time when we would be 'in the field'. In the meantime we had to endure six hours a day reading and inwardly digesting the *Blue Book*. It wasn't really a book at all but an elaborate file with a blue cardboard cover and a stick-on label saying 'SECRET – Property of the Bank of London and South America', BOLSA for short, which was handy for a Bank operating in South America because *Bolsa* happens to be the Spanish for stock exchange as well as handbag. The *Blue Book* was so secret that we were not allowed to remove it from the building. Why the secrecy, I wondered? Were we about to learn things that were not entirely on the level? The word SECRET might have been put on the cover just to capture our interest in the book's contents for longer than the first couple of days. It certainly gave me a *frisson* and stimulated my self-importance even more than my rolled-up umbrella and neatly folded *Times*. I might not have been able to talk about its sacred contents in the pub although I unashamedly bragged about its utter secrecy.

The book's joint authors were our two instructors, Mr Smythe and Mr Terence Thwaite (somehow we never learned Mr Smythe's first name). In stature Smythe, as we came to call him, was very like my father though that's where the similarity ended for he had none of my father's flair, dress sense or penchant for loud bow ties. Short, dumpy, overweight, size 17 inch collars and no neck to speak of, Smythe's suit was ill-fitting, the trousers too long and there was a crease below the jacket collar where the permanent stoop began. Shirts were nylon of the drip-dry, non-iron variety; never a stiff collar or a double cuff with the flash of a link, and always a Windsor-knotted tie with the top button showing. The shoes were immaculate, black and shiny with a spit-and-polish toe-cap such as befitted a successful city gent in the late sixties. But the shoes' incongruity served to highlight the humdrum nature of the rest of his garb: a grubby Gannex overcoat, pilled grey scarf, and a green wool trilby with a pheasant feather in the hat band on the side nearest the bow. The rest was as you would expect: a pronounced Estuary accent and a laugh that was no more than a series of short pants interspersed with brief high-pitched squeals. He laughed a lot at his own jokes:

'You'll soon get to know the local *señoritas* if you follow my meaning', and 'You lot are quite bright. I've 'ad trainees in the past who never got to know the difference between a debit and a credit'.

'What, Mr Smythe', we all chorused, 'is so funny about that?' The question stumped him so he told us again.

Memorable phrases he used on a daily basis which have burrowed into my sub-conscious include:

'Never trust anyone.'

(Odd, don't you think, Mr Smythe, a life without trust?)

'Don't reveal the contents of the Blue Book to local staff. You never can tell.'

(You never can tell what, Mr Smythe? Whether someone not born and educated in England can be trusted with a SECRET?)

'Remember you are ambassadors and have a duty to your shareholders.'

(OK, I was turned down by the Foreign Office but I know about shareholders: they read the City pages and smoke Balkan Sobranie).

'Never fail to wear suits and ties, particularly in the tropics, and invest in a tuxedo.'

(Actually, I rather fancied all that, and looked forward to it, though at the time I hadn't yet experienced the hot oven blast of tropical temperatures that kills at a stroke all sartorial inclinations).

His briefcase resembled more a dispatch box than a briefcase and was amply big enough to hold a dozen ledgers, a flask of tea (he never touched coffee), and a packet of digestive biscuits. 'Be prepared' he would say with a knowing wink which reminded me of a Boy Scout poster that used to hang in a heavy frame above my bed.

Smythe and Thwaite were chalk and cheese although both had followed identical careers in different countries. Occasionally the instruction would stop while they both reminisced about subjects as far removed as the idiosyncratic subtleties of Chilean and Brazilian banking law, and the journeys they had both undertaken to far-flung outposts in the pursuit of their duties. Initially uninspiring though these exchanges were they did allow us just a glimpse beyond our grey desk tops of the sun-filled horizons that awaited us on the other side of the Atlantic. We would be flying there in a matter of hours powered by jet engines but they spoke of two weeks by ship from Southampton to Rio; three to Valparaíso (with never an attempt to pronounce it correctly), hearing the samba of Brazil a little louder every day on the ship's radio, watching for when the crew changed into tropical gear, seeing the first flying fish. These anecdotes drove us on through the morass of Bank legislation and incomprehensible *Blue Book* jargon till we were in the pull and suck of an unknown world shortly to become home and which had to be more exciting than the murky City streets and the final remnants of the bowler-hatted gents queuing behind white lines at Waterloo for the Southern Railway underground train to Bank. I confess I had a bit of a soft spot for the bowler but didn't think of wearing one until it really was too late and I'd left the City for good.

Thwaite proudly showed us photographs of him walking down the street in Recife, also known as the 'Venice of the North' because of the waterways that run through the city. Other pictures showed him sitting at his manager's desk, or standing with black servants in front of the Bank, an imposing mock baroque façade with the Bank's coat of arms amusingly topped by a condor (South America's extremely rapacious bird of prey) above the door. He was wearing white linen suits of impeccable whiteness with deep creases on the arms and legs (I decided to get a couple made as soon as I arrived), stiff collar and perfect tie.

'Just the kit', he would say, 'for Re-syphilis, the Venereal of the North, as we always referred to it over G & T's in the British Club'.

Then he'd smack the back of his fingers in punishment for saying something so *risqué*. He was to the core a gentleman, an Old Etonian of the classic kind, erect, aloof, expensively dressed and groomed. There was just a hint of a moustache, bushy eyebrows and a short back and sides haircut that made his ears stick out comically which we were quick to comment on behind his back. For some reason he took a bit of a fancy to me, perhaps because I had now been told I was destined for Brazil, and introduced me to his barber in Cannon Street, just along from the now defunct silversmith's Mappin and Webb, who cut hair with a cut-throat razor and despatched rogue hairs with a lighted taper. Further down was his old-fashioned tailor (tape measure round the neck, huge scissors in a leather pouch at the waist, and gold half-moon spectacles on a chain) who was told to look after me 'nicely' and make sure I had plenty of ticket pockets. In the fitting room there were photographs all around of Winston Churchill being kitted out with unflattering baggy velvet suits by the self-same tailor which didn't augur well for my own.

We were constantly reminded by Smythe that he wrote the bulk of the *Blue Book* on board ship on his way home after retirement from 'the field' in Chile. Having worked as manager in most of the Chilean branches during a long and loyal career, Smythe was prevailed upon by the Staff Manager (no Human Resources in those days) to set down in writing every single one of the Bank's operations (some undertaking which would need to be tackled with significant doses of love which Smythe had in plenty) and then instruct roomfuls of hapless trainees using the book as a constant guide. There was a chapter on Kiting (an image suggesting, as far as I can remember, cheques that may or may not bounce), a Pig in a Poke (sadly no amusing reference here to Noel Coward's bounder 'who took to pig-sticking in quite the wrong way'), and a lengthy description of how to close down an established branch that had fallen victim to the constant vagaries of an inexpertly run South American economy. That the branch may have been poorly managed was never an option. You don't manage poorly if you commit your *Blue Book* to memory as all assiduous trainees should.

Each of us was issued with a ledger (dark blue board cover with 'Ledger' in gold letters, endless blue and pink lines on every page), and three blocks of vouchers, white, pink and yellow. Much of our day was spent filling in an amount on each voucher and then entering the same amount in the ledger in accordance with the *Blue Book*'s instructions on Double Entry Book Keeping (a subject understood only by masterful mathematicians with a special interest in finicky detail, an enviable ability to see the full picture, and then to delight in it). The vouchers acted as a sort of anaesthetic on my brain: I'd drift off in a daze then discover I had missed some vital piece of information without which further progress was impossible. I was constantly in a muddle, dropped my vouchers on the floor, and my sums didn't add up. One or two of the other trainees took to it instantly (they'd had the forethought and the brains to do Maths A level while I remained stuck at an E grade in O level). Debits (yellow vouchers) were entered on the left of the page because Smythe told us to put them on the window side of the ledger. Indeed, to my left were five windows with views over other windows on the opposite side of a narrow passage so no sunlight ever came into our room and there was no escape from the unutterably dull work on which we were engaged. The worst thing for me was that every day at 5 pm we had to hand in our ledger to Smythe who duly handed it back the next day having taken it home and marked it. I was convinced that I would soon be asked to leave but now that I'd tasted my first ever proper salary I no longer wanted that. Money definitely sweetened the bitter pill.

The pay for the time was astronomical for a chap just down from university, £1050 per annum, and was £100 more than my father's teaching salary in 1968, his last year of service after a lifetime in the profession. On top of that the Bank made generous contributions on my behalf into its own pension scheme which I have never benefited from as you had to stick it for a minimum of 6 years before acquiring any pension rights. There was also something called London Record which meant that your salary was converted into local currency when you were 'in the field' at four or five times its sterling value. I was told I would get even more local currency in Brazil which in those days was considered a hardship posting. Provided Smythe saw fit to keep me on I was likely to net a very goodly sum every month. That was value for utter boredom wasn't it? It was for a time, but it wasn't too many months before the attraction of a fat salary for what was in essence a very dull job, ceased to appeal.

Every Thursday those of us who were off to Brazil had an hour's language tuition from a tiny Portuguese woman called Dona Edith Oliveira. I suppose at the time there weren't enough suitably qualified Brazilians living in London who could have taught us: the exodus of musicians, artists and intellectuals from the military dictatorship (1964-85) was only just beginning in earnest. What I needed was the clear open-mouthed sounds of Brazilian Portuguese but what I got from Dona Oliveira was a few choice phrases full of the whooshes and sibilants of upper class Lisbon, and the words of a song which I occasionally still sing in the shower, full of mournful cadences about the mercifully permanent presence of bread and wine on a typical Portuguese table. I remember it all so clearly but the few words of the language I learned in London were to end up serving no practical purpose whatsoever. Once, Dona Edith's eyes filled with tears when we recited a silly English ditty we had made up on the way to the class: 'You will starve in the old Algarve'. She knew she was getting nowhere and began making excuses to miss classes.

With two weeks to go before our departure Smythe and Thwaite took their twelve charges to Farnham Castle for a two day conference on how to settle in to the South American way of life. It was exciting being out of the City, each in our own room, knowing we were at a 'Conference Centre'. We were addressed on the Argentine beef trade by a diplomat called Joint (one or two of us got the giggles and couldn't ask sensible questions afterwards). Then a very correct lady of a certain age told us how we should dress. Knowing looks from Smythe when she got to tuxedoes, ties, suits and the tropics. We dined in a huge hall with blackened beams each of us with thoughts racing about what lay in store, trying to find out what we could from the experienced person next to us. My neighbour, a lady, said 'Never eat salads – they are washed in polluted water'.

Thwaite took me to a side table where a young waitress was pouring coffees from an urn. 'Are these two little black ones free?' And then aside to me, 'They normally are in Brazil, you know', smacking the back of his fingers with a lingering smile. I still had a lot to learn about grown-up small talk.

We were advised to be guided by the well-tried recommendations of *The South American Handbook* hence my swift decision to secure my own copy. It was indeed a fund of information although some of the hints struck me even then as a trifle over-elaborate: 'The most suitable clothing for the tropics is either two or three light-weight suits of the "Palm Beach" type or, better still, half a dozen linen suits. A supply of thin cotton shirts, soft collars and light underwear are essential. At least one ordinary worsted or serge suit, and one suit of woollen underwear, will be required for high altitudes; a light overcoat is also useful for the same purpose. Evening dress is *de rigueur* for men at the opera.' I still have no clear idea precisely what was meant by a "Palm Beach" suit. There was an outfitters in Piccadilly, suitably named Tropiccadilly, and their extremely helpful shop assistant had no idea either so in the end I bought a couple of suits of their own manufacture. Detachable soft collars for tropical wear struck me as nothing short of instant torture. A book I was reading in preparation for my trip was H.W. Bates: *The Naturalist on the River Amazons* in which there was a graphic etching of the author 'Mobbed by curl-crested toucans', wearing what was obviously a shirt with a permanently attached collar. I assumed therefore that if he could, then so could I. I drew the line at worsted and serge, and assumed that the white tuxedo as favoured by Smythe would suffice if I ever had occasion to attend an opera.

My nice shop assistant then persuaded me to buy special shoes with breathable leather. In fact, there was nothing special about them apart from their provenance (again Tropiccadilly's own make) and their astronomical price. (They ceased to breathe as soon as they arrived).

My last few days were frantic. I made a lightning visit to Bentalls in Kingston (John Lewis was yet to corner the market) to acquire a navy blue trunk in which I packed all my clothes, a few books, a small battery operated portable Grundig tape recorder the size of a large dictionary, with as many classical tapes as I could afford, an enormous and very heavy free-standing loudspeaker with tweeter above to enhance the tinny sound of the Grundig, and an incongruous bottle of black Parker Quink ink which remained unopened for two years. I put the trunk on the train to Waterloo having pasted on it the Bank's address in Salvador, North East Brazil. It arrived eight weeks later covered in Lamport & Holt Shipping stickers and deep scratches, and when I triumphantly pushed back the lid it had been invaded by cockroaches.

With just a few days to go we were issued with a personal health form which we had to fill up and sign, and then show to the Bank's doctor before he conducted the medical. Two questions which took me by surprise were: 'Are there any signs of hernia? If so, is truss worn?'. When I arrived at the clinic I discovered that the doctor's name was Phelam, extremely appropriate for one who was about to conduct the 'Cough please' test for hernia. Why the Bank was so concerned that I might be suffering from such a complaint I never discovered, but Dr Phelam did his duty and passed me with flying colours. The *Handbook's* 'Hygiene and Health' section was reassuring:

'There is a large number of druggist shops where European and American medicaments can be bought. Epidemic diseases have been brought under control by public sanitation...Take a supply of purgatives (salts or pills). A superb intestinal bacteriostatic drug for the control of diarrhoea is *Entero-Vioform* (Ciba). A supply is essential for travellers in the tropics'.

Other general hygiene advice was not for the faint-hearted and I was pleased to have decided early on not to show the book to my parents. There is an entire paragraph devoted to essential 'simple' precautions that must be observed: 'Never sit in damp clothes, even for five minutes. Change as soon as you can after a hot journey. Don't take chilling showers. Be careful of the food. Don't eat surface vegetables or unpeeled fruit. Eat meals only when they are well cooked...."*Boeuf tartare*" should definitely be avoided'. How would I ever remember all this expert advice, I asked myself with some bewilderment. I derived scant reassurance from learning that 'Afternoon tea, made as it ought to be made, can be had in all the principal cities'.

With my departure date looming, there was oil to be poured on very troubled waters at home. During the three long months of the trainee course I had lived at home commuting daily to the City by train, the same aisle seat virtually every day, very much beholden to the railway timetable, while most of my colleagues splashed out their wages on a London flat and had tales to tell every morning during the coffee break. We knew I was to spend two uninterrupted years in Brazil but somehow pushed this knowledge to the back of our minds while the date still seemed far off. In those days of course two years meant exactly what it said. There were no cheap flights home and long distance telephone calls involved direct contact with an operator, an interminably long wait and crushing expense. It took hours to call a number even in neighbouring France and cost pounds every minute. We all knew that calls from Brazil were out of the question, that I could not fly home, and that our only link would be by letter. This was too much for my father to bear. Now that I am a father myself I can fully understand why, although at the time I considered he was being too emotional and more than a touch obstructive. Could I not ask to remain in London, he wondered, and climb up the ladder in England? My memories of the florid little National Provincial man opening my savings bank were enough to put paid to that one.

By now I was engaged to be married to Rosie, a means of sealing our relationship because the Bank strictly forbade trainees to marry during their first two years' absence 'in the field'. Despite all the genuinely joyful celebrations organised by my parents just before my departure this can only have reinforced the feeling that their son was well and truly set on a course of his own shortly to take him right out of their sphere of influence. Goodness knows what might happen to him over two years in a land that they had never really thought about before. 'Anywhere near Buenos Ayrs?' (pronounced as written), they enquired. They were right to be concerned but I already had my ticket and my trunk was on its way. The inevitability of my imminent departure preoccupied them both to such a great extent because this was the furthest that anyone in our family had ever travelled in peace time before. Photographs of my father taken at the time reveal a man with a worry and an inclination to bite the lower lip.

On top of all this neither parent approved of my sister's young man and they felt that in me they were losing a vital prop, a possible go-between, someone with the impetuousness of youth and the vigour somehow to put a stop to it. And yet nothing was further from my mind. My sister was older than me, perfectly capable of carving a future for herself without any preposterous interference from a younger sibling. Where had they got that from? So when the time came for goodbyes I was dry-eyed in the midst of utter parental despair. We embraced as if the 'plane were shortly to drop out of the sky and bearded bandits like Che Guevara could already be heard sharpening their knives in dangerous un-policed jungles. When I turned and waved before disappearing into Departures at Heathrow I suddenly thought I might not see them again and my heart leaped out to them. For the first time I feared what they were fearing. This was not like catching the Golden Arrow to Paris and staying, coddled and cocooned, with close family friends. The grim reality of being on my own in an entirely unknown land had hit me fair and square between the eyes.

I was cold and miserable on the flight, wrapped up in a British Caledonian blanket, assailed by guilt, missing Rosie terribly and dreading the looming months of separation (she had to finish her degree before joining me the following August), and contemplating with a mixture of controlled excitement, utter loneliness and fear the prospect of two years in an alien country described officially by my employers as a 'hardship post'. What on earth had I let myself in for?

I took my first gulp of tropical air, hot, humid and full of the buzz of unknown creatures when we had half an hour at Recife (a.k.a. Re-syphilis) for refuelling. A black and yellow double-carapaced wasp-like insect about three inches long settled on the back of my hand as I stood and gazed at the dark streak of tropical forest on the horizon. Back on the 'plane we were served strips of chilled paw paw, a sharp new taste from the other side of the world. Through the window nothing but the endless canopy of forest, a pin-prick of a clearing, the odd thought that an Indian might be watching us, staring at the glint of a passing god.

3

Brazil

So I was finally here, in Brazilian air space, heading towards the great urban sprawl of São Paulo. It was odd to think that Brazil at the time didn't figure much in anyone's experience. Older generations in my family had heard of Rio de Janeiro where, so they mistakenly believed, the people spoke Spanish, but they would be hard pushed to pinpoint it on a map. Their comparative ignorance made me feel all the more like a pioneer. Brazil, fifth in size after Russia, Canada, China and the United States, probably because it was in South America, a continent that in the 1960s was largely unfamiliar, had gone relatively unnoticed. And yet in 1944, only twenty five years before my arrival, Brazil had been the only South American country to send an expeditionary force to help the Allied cause in Italy. It was a sizeable force (25,700) which took 20,573 enemy prisoners in total including the entire 148th Infantry Division. Local historians quite understandably like to think that the Brazilian contribution to the Allies hastened the end of the war. The 948 Brazilian dead are not commemorated in Britain, but in 1960 a magnificent and very moving memorial was built in a prominent position in Rio's Flamengo Park.

I had read somewhere that 'Brazil is the country of the future, and always will be'. Historians informed us that Brazilians had a propensity to develop industries that looked promising for a while and then went bust. Rubber and sugar had boomed until smart competitors set up elsewhere in similar climates and it was simply a matter of time before Brazil's market outlets collapsed. Foreign banks granted dollar and sterling loans which were automatically renewed when they fell due but which could stifle development whilst the banks regularly remitted huge profits to their Head Offices.

And yet there was a buzz in the larger cities where some of the expanding middle classes could draw salaries which allowed them to build and live in stylish high rise blocks. The most fortunate members of Brazilian high society had the penthouse on the top floor with a swimming pool and tall palm trees in heavy terracotta pots for shade. In fifty years Copacabana beach was transformed from virgin jungle to a sophisticated high rise suburb and now looks upon itself more as a separate city with its own identity rather than a suburb of Rio. In the late 1950s they bulldozed Santo Antonio's hill, dumped the earth along seven kilometres of shoreline, created a new beach, a park with numerous football pitches and spaces for leisure, and ran a dual carriageway spanned by handsome, delicate footbridges from Copacabana to the centre of Rio. In the same decade they started to build from the air Costa and Niemeyer's revolutionary bow-and-arrow-shaped capital city,

Brasília (now a World Heritage site), while disgruntled Indians shot arrows at the men working on the main roads leading to it. Understandably, foreign embassies were initially loath to leave their grand airy buildings and well-established shady gardens for the brash modern quarters in the new capital and held out for as long as they could in the sophisticated old world of Rio, but in the end of course they had to go.

As some grew very rich others, the vast majority, were confined to the burgeoning slums that sprang up next door to luxurious, shiny new developments. A strong dose of national pride and a confirmed belief that Brazil would always win the World Cup led the way forward. The poor unquestioningly paid a few cents more purchase tax to fund the national team's successes and spent the evening happily watching soap operas that exposed the moral turpitude of the wealthy. In 1969 Brazil's car and shop windows were covered with little stickers in the national colours saying 'Brazil: Love it or Leave it, and the last to leave turns out the lights'. But the economy was slowly growing and the days of 100% inflation were over for good. The old adage about Brazil always being the country of the future only lasted about a hundred years.

4

Salvador

São Paulo was a muddle of ugly streets, congestion and pollution, meeting bigwigs in smart offices high in the sky with views to the other side of the street, handshakes and wishes of good luck from middle-aged executives in well-tailored suits. My hotel (since bulldozed and replaced) was an ageing high-rise sporting ferrous stains on the façade with views across and beyond an iron bridge. I ate prawns in the restaurant because I could just about manage that in Portuguese without eliciting looks of blank incomprehension from the waiters. I woke in the middle of the night to the clank and screech of heavy metal and the regular drum-beat of hobnail boots. I stood by my window for an hour witnessing a whole army of tanks, guns and marching men flowing down the avenue, ignoring red lights, crossing the bridge and disappearing in the distant gloom. Was this the army rising up on behalf of the people against the fierce dictators who now ran the country? None of the waiters wanted to answer that at breakfast, or perhaps they genuinely didn't understand my faltering Portuguese. The hotel manager told me in laboured English that I must have imagined it. The newspapers in the lounge seemed not to mention it.

Later that day I was on my way to Salvador da Bahia de Todos os Santos, so named by Amerigo Vespucci who put in to the enormous bay for the first time on All Saints Day, 1st November 1501. He later gave his name to the entire southern continent which was called America well before the name was adopted further north. Much later it was claimed that Salvador had a different church for every day of the year (not true, in fact there are only 70) hence another reason for calling it 'Saviour of The Bay of All The Saints' but the airport in the 1960s simply had 'Salvador-Bahia' painted in white letters on the outside of a single one-storey concrete building.

The Bank factotum, a man in his forties with glasses as thick as the bottom of a beer bottle, was standing at a makeshift barrier clutching a paper with *Banco de Londres* scrawled on it in hollow capital letters filled in with lurid blue biro, an ink colour with which I was to become very familiar. Over the years he must have got used to meeting wide-eyed youths with tell-tale northern European alabaster brows because it was he who made the initial move and tugged at my sleeve. I hadn't yet linked *Banco de Londres* with the longer, more formal, and, as it turned out, impossible for Brazilians to pronounce, Bank of London and South America, so checking, and double checking that he was from the right Bank (little did I know at this stage that it was virtually the only Bank in town), I climbed into a gleaming Panhard and allowed him to take me where he would.

The Bank loomed large and important on one of the

wider avenues in the old commercial district and, oh bliss, had just undergone a thorough refit that included the installation of air-conditioning. I had missed the re-opening launch by a matter of hours so the first thing that greeted me was a pile of party detritus completely blocking one of the two glass doors. The second thing that struck me, and this was initially very strange because the outside temperature was in the upper thirties, was that the staff behind the counter were wearing shawls and blankets to counter the newly-installed air conditioning to which they were totally unaccustomed. A quick word with the manager, a Brazilian with a surname that sounded suspiciously like the Spanish for hot red chilli pepper, another hand-shake and I was off in the car (not automatically provided with air-conditioning in those days) to settle in to my flat. Manuel das Neves do Nascimento (Manuel of the Birth Snows), for thus was the driver called, lost no time in telling me that Jesus had been born on a cold snowy night which explained his mother's choice of name, and that my block of flats had just won a prestigious architecture prize. All in the same breath at break-neck speed without a pause in between. When I had finally understood him we laughed and this was the start of a good relationship: Birth Snows and I, mastering my first smatterings of the language, had hit it off.

It was difficult to ascertain why my building had been awarded an Architecture prize. Perhaps it was because the building's façade followed an elliptical curve which permitted each flat to have its own particular view of the huge bay which featured in the name of the city. The un-prizeworthy ground floor was dominated by parked cars, flying footballs kicked by gangs of children, and over-spilling dustbins, and there were lifts up to the flats with just the beginning of graffiti on the mahogany veneer doors. Near the dustbins and out of sight was the service lift with several layers of different-coloured graffiti on the metal doors.

And then the first of many terrible shocks to my system: Birth Snows opened my front door on the seventh floor: 'Fuck Off!' came shrilly from within. 'Fuck Off... Fuck Off,' said with a marked degree of vehemence. Behind the door was a dusty and mangy parrot chained to a perch with empty water and food bowls. It flapped, ruffled its neck feathers and out of its pincer beak lolled a dry grey tongue. When I filled its water bowl it drank deep and long giving me the full impact of its flat yellow-black eye. It had been abandoned a week previously by my predecessor and was lucky to have survived. Its name as I learned later, was indeed Fuck Off, and that sadly was the limit of its vocabulary. What heartless person could have inflicted the last few days of drought and starvation on it? And who, apart from the permanently drunk and idle, would have christened it thus? I was getting my first glimpse of how seriously Smythe's smart young men took upon themselves the burden of flying the flag.

Word of my arrival spread quickly. I heard someone with a key opening the back door that led into the kitchen via the maid's quarters. She introduced herself as Valdete (pronounced Val det chee), told me my predecessor had sacked her so as not to pay for her food in the intervening week, and would I be so kind as to offer her her old job back? Birth Snows nodded approval. Valdete was a simple soul, still in her teens, who believed that all foreigners drank heavily, wasted food and were American. I drew a rudimentary map including the US and Europe but she glazed over and couldn't follow what I said.

Did I mind the stains on the kitchen wall near the ceiling? They were too high for her to reach and had been there for months, the lasting legacy of Senhor Alan who brought a whore to the flat and amused her by smashing eggs from the 'fridge high up against the wall. I was to be haunted for two years by other people's stories of the doings of Senhor Alan for he left trails of destruction and unhappiness wherever he went. His last posting was to Maceió just a few hundred miles up the coast from Salvador. Predictably enough he knocked a woman off her bike injuring her horridly, then misbehaved with the only daughter of a family of four siblings who came seeking their revenge. He was drinking on the terrace of a bar just opposite the Bank when the three brothers drew up in a car and emptied their handguns into him. When news of his death filtered down to Salvador the local staff exchanged a number of knowing glances that made it only too clear that he'd had it coming to him. A pretty clerk in her thirties called Darcy was rumoured to have had a fleeting but life-changing affair with him that left her wounded to the quick with a lasting distrust of men, particularly the well-scrubbed ones from England, that came and went with their urgent appetites demanding short-lived pleasure and instant gratification. We had a dreadful reputation to live down. I need hardly say that neither Senhor Alan's untimely demise nor my parrot's unseemly name was reported in my first letter home. But I sent a detailed account to Rosie whose reply contains some measure of understatement:

A scream about the parrot's name. Surely you'll have to try teaching it to say something else? Glad you were able to rescue it but I foresee problems transporting it around Brazil as you change postings – on a chain somehow attached to your shoulder like Long John Silver?

I have checked on the map and Maceió appears to be hundreds of miles from Salvador, and that poor man, what a way to go, and so young, but interesting to learn how Brazilian families can take the law into their own hands. I can only assume this was an isolated incident and that Bank staff are quite safe. BOLSA wouldn't send anyone anywhere that wasn't, would they? Probably best not to mention it to your parents who are certain to worry...

The male clerks in the Bank were made of sterner stuff and secretly admired trainees like Senhor Alan that were quick to get themselves known for loutishness and sexual misdemeanours. Carlos in charge of current accounts had a bright orange card for each customer on a revolving wheel which he claimed made it easier for him to find individual accounts. A quick turn of the handle was all that was required. In the top right hand corner of each card he had pencilled figures each with a slight variation on the one before so that as he turned the wheel you could watch matchstick men and women lewdly involved with one another. Only male clerks knew about this and guffawed with monotonous regularity towards the end of the day when account cards had to be brought up to date. I was considered unmanly for not wanting to be part of this although whenever

I caught a glimpse of the matchsticks' shenanigans I privately thought how well executed they were.

Walter, who proudly told me to my face that he was also known as Gillette, the blade that cuts both ways, varnished his nails and wore eye make-up which at the time was extremely daring although I doubt whether the dashing Brazilian manager or his bull-necked English deputy noticed very much from behind the closed doors of their offices. He once showed me the paintings he had done over the years, each the size of a post card, but he was wary of his feminine side and found the taunts of his colleagues difficult to bear. I admired him for looking upon the Bank (as did I) merely as a source of income which permitted him in the evenings and at weekends to lead another life. His flat was full of shades of purple, cushions and hangings, with square holes in the walls instead of windows, and angular abstract paintings on the walls. His front door led on to a small patio with potted plants that provided some cool shade. Everything said permanence and belonging, the very opposite of my existence in my grand award-winning flat with its standard issue plastic furniture and utilitarian crockery. I didn't even own a potted plant and what's worse, didn't at the time think a potted plant was important given that I was only there for a few months anyway. I found it very difficult indeed feeling at home in a flat that had been poorly furnished and well abused by others.

Sampaio of Foreign Exchange was respectably married with a number of children who used to come with their mother at closing time and wait for him quietly in the delectable air-conditioned cool of the foyer. Whenever I rang him on the internal phone, or delivered a document to his desk, he would whisper his only English words, gleaned no doubt from a past trainee, with a wicked grin showing beneath his full moustache: 'Kiss my balls', which he pronounced 'Kees', and he knew what it meant too. This happened several times a day. To keep him sweet I had to smile, reassure him I wouldn't say anything to the manager and utter meaningless words such as 'yes Sampaio, you are fluent in English', or 'O Sampaio, you are a one'.

The ladies were, as ladies always are, much more demure and I owed to them my first forays into Portuguese because they took the time and trouble, and considerable pride, to teach me to pronounce and speak the language accurately. If ever we went up the stairs together to the second floor where the typists worked the ladies insisted I went up first; when we returned downstairs they had to go first. The reason for this extraordinary reversal of what I was used to in England was quite simple and had been imposed upon them over the many years of working in what was essentially a male-dominated environment. If a man went behind them up the stairs he could (and in this country definitely would) look up their skirts. Ditto if he preceded them down the self-same stairs.

Brazilian social skills belong to a class of their own. Customers would enter the Bank, spot me sitting at my desk, get my attention by hissing '*P-siu*' as loud as they could through pursed lips, then beckon me to the front. During the ensuing conversation they would lean an elbow on the counter and deftly undo all my shirt buttons. This was very disarming the first couple of times that it happened but I soon got quite used to it. I knew the conversation was at its end when they slipped a hand inside my shirt, slapped me on the torso and said '*Está gordo*' ('You're fat'), a great compliment in the Brazilian business world. In restaurants, if the food is good they pinch their ear lobes and say '*Ô*'; if it's very, very good, they extend their right arm behind their head, pinch the left ear lobe and say '*Ô, Ô*' more loudly. To suggest speed or urgency, for example when describing a police chase in pursuit of a criminal gang, the entire Brazilian nation seems to have developed from birth the remarkable skill of leaving limp the fingers of the right hand which, when raised and lowered in quick succession, produce an emphatic clicking sound somewhat akin to the sound of running feet. I am convinced that no-one other than a Brazilian can do this.

A little old Englishwoman with alert blue eyes and a grimy backpack would ride in to Salvador regularly every fortnight and hitch her horse to an iron ring sunk incongruously into the wall by the Bank's sliding glass door, then demand to see her money. She had a sizeable account, the equivalent in local currency of £25,000 which in 1969 would have purchased a small flat in Eaton Square. The cashier knew her well and would groan inwardly as he contemplated yet again the prospect of counting out this sum so he eventually came to keep in a corner of the safe a cardboard box with 'her' money in it. And so it went on for some months until the day he forgot, or just didn't bother, to get her to sign for it. When he looked up she was no longer in her usual place, on the green leather sofa by the door, but had vanished into thin air taking the money with her. The following day she returned, demanded her money, signed for it this time, and was never seen again. She probably bought a large flat in Eaton Square while the unfortunate cashier saw most of his income every month disappear as the Bank tried to recoup its losses. One of the sections in the *Blue Book* dealt with just such an occurrence and explained how much the Bank could fairly deduct from the cashier's wages which were by all standards pretty low. This was probably one of the reasons why the *Blue Book* needed to retain its secrets from local staff and share nothing with anybody. Such grossly unfair treatment no doubt kept the distant shareholders happy.

There were three other English people living in my award-winning building, all a little older than me. Rodney had completed his two years as a trainee and had recently been promoted to branch Accountant which meant overseeing all the business and maintaining 'good banking practice', a phrase filched direct from the *Blue Book*. He also had overall responsibility for staff, particularly English staff, on whom he wrote regular reports on pink air mail paper that went in the Bank bag straight to London. I cannot imagine the moral criteria he brought to bear as he plotted our progress for he must have considered his own precarious lifestyle was the only way forward. Birth Snows was given the important job of driving the bag to the airport, waiting until the British Caledonian crew arrived, and then handing the bag to the pilot. The Bank's branches all over South America must have had similar arrangements with air crews because news left and arrived remarkably quickly.

Rodney, along with many other ex-pats, lived a double life. At work he was smart, sharp and knew all the answers but as soon as his day was done, the other, darker side of his personality emerged. In the evenings and at weekends he was in a permanent state of drunkenness shouting obscenities at waitresses and barking at taxi drivers to take him to No. 63. This was a brothel on the road lined with crumbling colonial terraced houses that linked the lower city, where the Bank and other international businesses were located, with the upper city from which there were striking views over the bay. He told me to accompany him there once since he was too drunk to stand. A more seedy and unpleasant establishment would be hard to find anywhere: broken, filthy furniture; diseased young girls some of whom can't have been more than ten; an overpowering *Senhora* wearing a greasy turban and brandishing a stick. Rodney spent his weekend evenings there and was often a visitor during the week. I recall one evening when the Bank Manager wanted him on urgent business and we knew exactly where to find him.

For some reason he had a key to my flat and would let himself in at all hours with or without his paramour for the night and help himself to the spare bedroom and whatever he could find in the kitchen. Other people therefore, complete strangers of the lowest sort off the street, were allowed to finger my things and drink the contents of my 'fridge. It was a wonder I was never burgled. On many mornings I was obliged to breakfast with his previous night's companion then unlock the door and let her out. On one occasion when he did get up, he steered her out of the flat, unclipped the haplessly-named parrot from its perch, went down to his car and drove off, his left arm out of the window with the parrot clutching his forefinger for dear life, his lady friend laughing uncontrollably at his side. The inevitable happened: the bird flew in the direction of the jungle and was never seen again. I doubt very much whether he survived the rest of the day.

Never a word from Rodney who continued his mad lurchings without a thought for those in his entourage. And yet he had had a privileged education: a leading Public School followed by Greats at Oxford. In two and a half years in Brazil he had kicked over all the traces of those years of care and nurture. He had now become a very ordinary individual with selfish pursuits and ambitions to walk tall fired with drink and to wallow in self-indulgence. And the loneliness was catching up with him. Already in his mid twenties, he knew that a long-lasting relationship would never be his to enjoy and that he was on the brink of the chasm of solitude with the prospect of a life unfulfilled and with no meaning.

Nigel and Sam completed the picture. They matched Rodney drink for drink but drew the line at No. 63, unable, as indeed was I, to comprehend what he found so alluring about it. A favourite haunt was the British Club, a nineteenth century single storey ivy-clad building in the upper city, overlooking a broad, airy square. The qualification for membership was being an upper middle class *Bahiano* (which excluded all the local staff in the Bank), or an Englishman. Americans and Dutch were tolerated, just, but only because they were foreign. There was an outside terrace with lightweight wicker chairs and soft cushions, air mail editions of the *Times* dating back some weeks, and electric fans on the ceiling. Inside was the bar with heavier leather furniture, a colour poster of the young Queen Elizabeth, and a framed black and white photograph of Churchill complete with cigar and Victory salute. At one end was a wicker screen behind which profligate young ex-pat men with a full range of sexually transmitted diseases, who worked for various international firms represented in the city, would consult Dr Lima, a thin-moustached middle-aged Brazilian with a permanent twinkle in his eye. His fee for each prescription was a round of drinks and his only English was the names of the different complaints that his patients brought him.

Sam was a telephone engineer and manager of Western Telegraph, a square functional building crammed full of what looked to me like Edwardian telephone equipment: brass, spark-generating gadgets on mahogany bases inside glass cases as if on display in an exhibition. But this was for real. Western Telegraph 'phones were not for private individuals, only for businesses, and every time someone in the city picked up the heavy black bakelite receiver they got straight through to the Western Telegraph switchboard, a *Bahiana* with a husky voice and absolutely no English. The 'phones could only be used for sending telegrams with each word in the message spelled out separately in accordance with locally chosen words beginning with the required letter. So 'regards' would be *Raquel Eduardo Goiás Ana Raquel David Salvador*. You can imagine how long it took to send a telegram, and there was no question of her reading it back so you could check she had noted everything correctly. It was all very quaint and faintly disturbing. The operator, moreover, had no sense of humour. I signed one telegram home with my initial P, but instead of saying Paulo I very stupidly (just for a laugh) and unwisely (O the utter foolishness of wanting to find out if she could spell), said *Pneumonia* which, in an unusual departure from the norm, the operator spelled out perfectly correctly in full, and this had my parents up in arms thinking I was at death's door. Their panicky letters in response took three weeks to arrive and my replies took three more weeks, so they lived for six weeks with no news of their dying son. I decided not to send another telegram on the grounds that cryptic messages such as 'Still alive' or 'Not dead don't worry' would do more harm than good, and that they would be sensible enough to believe the old dictum that no news was almost certainly good news. But of course, as it turned out, I had forgotten their considerable capacity for worry.

There were a few other odd ex-pats dotted around the city, mainly Danes in the tobacco trade, who regularly accompanied us to bars and restaurants and had a powerful northern European inclination towards the bottle. They would organise meals in the Danish style: twenty small dishes with tiny portions, schnapps out of the freezer (a novelty for me) and beer, then silly rules obliging their unsuspecting guests to consume far too much alcohol in the Danish style or be struck off their list. The ex-pat community was made up of a motley collection of individuals all thrown together, forced to live with each other's foibles, attaching undue importance to insignificant developments, such as the opening of a new Chinese restaurant called the *Tong Fong*. Brazilians could only pronounce it *Tong-y Fong-y* and within a short while taxi drivers were soon chuckling about how the local pronunciation sounded like a Chinaman with a strong accent saying 'I'm hungry' in Portuguese.

These minor diversions held us together like glue and kept us amused although they concealed the utter superficiality that drove us to do and say the things we did. Nigel, Sam and others lived in a little tropical England. Sunk in the worn leather armchairs of the British Club they concerned themselves with the parlous state of the British cemetery decaying behind its broken metal gate, awaited like eager schoolboys the April start of the English cricket season, and bemoaned socialism and Harold Wilson's latest blunders. On July 20th 1969 they listened to the Moon Landings on a short wave radio in the car park in front of the Club. The 'small step' and the 'giant leap' were cheered with gin and tonic and a slice of lime. I never saw them walking through the vibrant *Modêlo* market and they knew nothing of the throb of African drums down by the old harbour. The sweet scent of burning herbs coming from windows, and the acrid smell of *dendê* oil frying *acarajé* doughnuts on every street corner passed them by.

Taxi drivers had to be treated with a good deal of respect because many were in the pay of the secret police and discussion about politics and particularly the brutality of the police was strictly not allowed. There were stories about people mysteriously going missing, victims of the *esquadrão da morte* (death squad) who roamed the streets in white vans picking up suspects who were never seen again. Small street children, considered by the authorities a blot on the city's reputation, were said to be rounded up late at night, put out of their misery with a shot to the head, placed on a sliding tray in a baker's van then dumped in the municipal land-fill site on the outskirts of town. Of course none of this could be reported in the press. We all knew when the censor had been at work because the *Jornal do Brasil*, a national broadsheet, filled the censor's gaps pretty well every day with verses of *Os Lusíadas*, the sixteenth century Portuguese epic poem by Luis de Camões. It was said at the time that the lengthy poem had already been fully reprinted by the newspaper three and a half times in the four years since the military dictatorship began in 1964. The censors either tolerated this or were ignorant of its importance to the newspaper's readers.

I suppose we all got used to the blithe way in which the authorities dealt with undesirable elements among the local population and we just put up with it for the sake of our own safety. It was vital to stay on the right side of the police and we often left a late-night bar prematurely if there was a rumour on the street that the police, always armed to the teeth, were on the prowl. One memorable morning I arrived at the Bank to see on the pavement under the windows a homeless woman looking to all intents and purposes as if she were asleep. I thought no more of it for the homeless were commonplace in the city and begged for food and money wherever they could before being moved on, often brutally, by the police. At lunchtime, however, there was a lighted candle on the pavement next to her; at Bank closing time there were a dozen, and a small group of people had gathered chatting quietly amongst themselves. As I stood and watched, a dustcart with upward sliding doors along the sides came into view. One of the dustmen pitchforked the body as if it were a bale of straw into the cart which then drove off down the street. None of the bystanders had anything to say.

The same sort of nonchalance was in abundance at the zoo to which I went, keen to experience glimpses of the animals and insects that dwelt in the real jungle just a few miles from the outskirts of the city. At the gate there was a hole in the wall where you queued to buy your ticket, and next to it a little wooden hut where, for a few pennies, parents could buy a bag of stones for their children who were then encouraged to pelt the animals. As I write this I find it very hard to believe, but I have a very clear memory of the snake pit full of dazed snakes of varying species lying amid piles of pebbles and being pelted by small boys held securely over the edge by their fathers.

Distressing and gloomy though this was there were plenty of other things to cheer me up. My first Carnival was quite an eye opener. Lorries covered in colourful streamers bore samba bands each vying with the other to make the loudest noise and attract the greatest number of followers. One was called the *Trio Eléctrico* with three musicians each on the electric guitar, blaring their music through banks of megaphones attached to both sides of the lorry. The din was simply frightful but your pulse raced and your ribcage throbbed in time with the beat. On an open air stage gorgeous girls strutted from side to side attracting lewd shouts and frantic applause. Someone told me they were all men but the disguise was so perfect you really couldn't tell the difference. Walter (a.k.a. Gillette) told me later that he had seen me in the crowd from his vantage point as a performer on the stage and what a shame it was I hadn't recognised him.

A pall of gloom descended over the city and people began to wear black arm bands as news filtered through of the death of one of the greatest samba singers of all time, Ataulfo Alves, who died just before his 60th birthday after a bungled operation on an ulcer. The *Jornal do Brasil* reported that the whole country, including the deep south where there were mainly European immigrants and precious few descendants of African slaves, went into mourning that lasted some weeks. The mournful cadences of his songs could be heard in all the streets, bars and restaurants, and eventually someone brought a turntable and set it up in the Bank foyer. The poignant words of one of his songs had come true and as people came in off the street to listen there were tears in their eyes.

'I know I'm going to die.
I don't know the day or the time.
But when I die I want to die
To a lovely cadence of samba'.

Samba was everywhere and you couldn't fail to respond to its intoxicating rhythms. A man standing at the bar tapped with a finger on a box of matches; someone else replied with one glass clinking against another; a third would take up a knife and fork, and soon the bar rocked and swayed to a loud percussion that had passers-by holding their arms in the air and shuffling along the street, their bodies moving with natural grace in time to the beat. Ataulfo was mourned in every city of the land by people who got up like this and performed their own individual tributes. You couldn't help but be part of it as it gradually seeped into your soul. When they saw you responding to the beat they shouted 'Opa', asked if you liked it then grinned from ear to ear. Part of me was enjoying the sensation of moving like them and with them, and they were flattered to bits that a foreigner should get so involved.

All this was known in the Bank and soon reached the manager who, with a gesture of stunning generosity, said I could have the Panhard at weekends. My newly-won friend Birth Snows didn't go with it as driver so with a certain amount of trepidation (in fact I was utterly terrified) I ventured out of the City up a road that soon became a track and drove into the interior towards the first town of any size on the map, Feira de Santana, where there is a permanent market for goods from the remotest corners of the State. There were leather crops and whips; clusters of three solid leather balls at the end of a long thong that you swung round your head like a lassoo then let go in order to catch your cattle; brown, cream and black hides; crude metal stirrups; wooden bowls hollowed with chisels; small terra cotta dishes that I had seen in the city on corners full of food offerings no doubt to the gods about whom at the time I knew nothing. Rice, beans and manioc flour were in huge white leather chests on the ground.

Gliding north the following weekend on freshly laid tarmac towards Maceió I thought I might even get there for lunch but the smart highway maddeningly soon turned to dirt, then the rain bucketed and I was forced to leave the impassable track to one side and bump uneasily across country fearing all the while for the Panhard's suspension and worrying about bushes scratching the paintwork. The petrol gauge was low and I knew I was lost for I had strayed too far from the road. The sun was still hidden behind clouds so there was no chance of being sure I was pointing north and all the time the needle sank lower and lower. At last, there loomed into my field of vision a man on a horse. He looked like something out of a Western movie with his cowboy hat and a rifle resting in a pouch slung from the saddle, his horse bedecked with dusty red and yellow tassels between the ears. When I enquired how far away the next village was he replied:

'Two and a half leagues'.

I then asked if he knew of a garage where I could get petrol but he looked perplexed when I said the word *gasolina*. I got out, opened the bonnet, pointed at the engine and said once again *gasolina*. His response was, and as I write this I can hardly believe it myself:

'Does your horse need something to eat?'

I followed the rump of his horse as the dusk came down wondering what on earth I would do if the petrol did finally run out for I had no supplies in the car, no water, nothing. But at least he was honest and kind because he led me in the right direction and I was soon back on the slithery road with a petrol station round the next bend, so the story has a happy though anti-climactic ending.

This was my first encounter with someone who appeared to belong to a different era, and whose lifestyle was entirely different from my own. I wondered where he was from and what sort of house he lived in. Perhaps he was a nomad who had made this scrubland his home and had been disturbed by the road builders. I little knew at the time that within a couple of years my life would change drastically and encounters with men and women like this would become quite common, while memories of my previous life as a Bank trainee preparing for the glamorous world of high finance receded into the distance.

My days in the Bank were filled mostly with finger-strumming boredom as I had next to nothing to do. I promised myself early on that I would not remain long in the Bank. The little I was learning in a section enticingly called *Ordens e Pagamentos* (Orders and Payments), written in silver on a black plastic stand beside my typewriter, convinced me that I was probably better suited to a calling outside banking. The clerks who were supposed to show me the ropes had their own work for which they were paid a pittance to get through every day, and quite understandably they didn't relish having to spend time teaching me their job. They felt that everything I did needed to be checked anyway so they tended to look upon me as a waste of their time. I sat and looked while they busied themselves with the daily chores. They never showed it but deep down they must have resented my earning so much more than them and doing nothing to deserve it. Trainees were supposed to sit, watch and learn like this for two years before getting their first promotion. The boredom factor needle spun out of control every day because every day the monotony was worse. There were occasional moments, a little like the splash of cold water on a hot day, that reminded me there was more to life than coloured vouchers, but they were rare and when they happened they impressed themselves upon my memory.

One such afternoon, outlined against the glass doors, sunburned and peeling with sun-bleached hair, an obviously English-looking couple stood counting out foreign notes on the counter. They had just arrived in a small sailing boat having sold their farm for cash in Kenya some weeks before and the notes they were trying to change were the old-fashioned black and white fivers that hadn't been in circulation for years but were still legal tender. They invited me to their boat for the evening and met me down in the harbour with their dinghy at 5 pm. Unsuitably be-suited I climbed aboard and we rowed out towards a tiny boat, no more than 25 feet long, bobbing in the middle of the harbour. The cabin accommodation was decidedly cramped and I had a cupboard door handle right in the small of my back so they opened the door to make me more comfortable. The cupboard was stuffed full of old-fashioned fivers and they showed me other cupboards just as full. After a simple dinner (the first fresh vegetables they had had for a long time) we lay sprawled on the deck, glass in hand, looking across the water at the two levels of the shimmering city, hearing the beat of samba and the occasional car horn. We stayed there for hours, chatting away, exchanging stories. I decided I wouldn't go home but would go straight on to the Bank from here in the morning and force myself to get through the day. At three or four in the morning when the hubbub of the city had dwindled to a minimum we heard a silvery trombone playing slow, mournful blues pierce the night air and come floating towards us over the water, every note, although very distant, crystal clear. We determined to find the musician who was producing such a wonderful sound, so back into the dinghy we climbed and made our way towards a barnacled metal ring in the harbour wall. I guessed roughly where we should head: the notorious street that joined the lower and upper cities with Rodney's favourite No. 63 half way up it. The first dilapidated colonial buildings overlooking the sea were just beginning to be restored, the crumbling insides gutted with the façades left intact, and through one of the windows, standing on a pile of rubble, eyes scrunched tight, playing his heart out in the direction of Africa, was our man. A few solitary drinkers sat listening at tables in a makeshift bar that had arisen out of the ruins. We stayed there, not talking now but entranced by this extraordinary solo performance until the sun came up and I had to hasten away.

Another chance visitor, bringing the dazzle of São Paulo fashion and an endearing smile into the Bank one Friday afternoon, was the strikingly beautiful Katia, the daughter of a Brazilian mother and English father, on holiday in the North East, determined to see the sights. She persuaded me to accompany her on Saturday to Itaparica, an island in the Bay which could be seen from the mainland lying dark and mysterious on the horizon. She knew a bit of its history. The slave ships passed it on their way to Salvador leaving firmly imprinted in the minds and memories of their unhappy cargo that it was the only land mass along this stretch of coast where the sun could (almost) set over the sea, a vital part of Yoruba burial rites. Most of the slaves never set foot on it but some after liberation settled here and established a secret cult of the dead. We would have no chance of getting anywhere near the cult house (I had to wait another two years before I could do this) but it would be fun to negotiate a lift in a fisherman's boat and see what we could of the island.

All went well until the time came to return. We squatted with the fishermen in a circle on the beach, the distant sky above Salvador showing a smear of oily brown pollution whilst the wind got up and white horses appeared on the sea. There was a storm in the air and they weren't prepared to risk it. Mr Miller, the silent and brooding English exile who ran the island's only hotel, gave us a couple of rooms. We drank *caipirinha*, the lethal raw sugar cane brandy drink that at the time was subject to two taxes when imported in to England: alcohol and a separate duty payable on poison. A single drink does no harm, but a second guarantees a raging headache. Only fools contemplate having a third. Then we dined on curried eggs and salad (at Farnham Castle I had been told never to touch salad which would almost certainly have been washed in unfiltered water, and the water in this hotel's taps came out grey). There was plenty of banter the following day among my group of friends about how I had managed to entice the delectable Katia to a remote island for the night and get her to drink *caipirinha*. Suggestive tittle tattle like this was the staff of life for those who spent most evenings and weekends at the British Club calling for more gin with ice up to the rim of the glass, consulting the doctor and rustling outdated cigarette-paper-thin airmail editions of the *Times*.

It was Katia who subsequently arranged for me to play host, along with a couple of anthropologists, to two Indians whose tribe, the *Patajós*, had been contacted in the southernmost part of the State of Bahia only a couple of years previously. This was to be their first excursion out of the jungle and in to the big City. Some missionaries had already taught them the rudiments of so-called civilised living: how to dress in tee shirt and jeans; the intricacies of the knife and fork; the chair and the table. But nothing could adequately prepare them for the lift with sliding doors up to the seventh floor. I needed to go and come several times, poking my head out of my window and waving, before they could be enticed into it. They were frightened of the great height from the window and needed to wash having met new friends. The sight of water coming from the taps left them in a state of utter bewilderment. One of them said that only that morning 'our women walked three kilometres and brought us water as always'. Lunch went off without much of a mishap until the pudding, an oval dish piled high with ice-cream, was set in the centre of the table. This was an unfortunate experiment dreamed up by the anthropologists who wanted to see what their reaction would be to food that clearly was steaming and yet wasn't hot. Their reaction was only too predictable and the ice cream delivered a cruel shock to their system. They then went off in a car to look at traffic and swimming pools. Precisely what the anthropologists got out of all this apart from a cheap thrill at seeing the simple world of the Indian turned upside down in such a brutal way, I do not know. Naturally I did find meeting and being with the Indians extremely exciting and it was almost certainly this that made me start to think I was wasting too much time on trivialities and that there were other far more important things that demanded my attention.

My visit to Alagados slum caused a number of middle-class eyebrows to twitch because, as everyone pointed out to me after the event, no-one in their right mind would risk it. Originally it must have been a glorious lagoon with an exit to the sea, but now most of its surface was covered with wooden piles driven into the water with many acres of township built on top. The more desirable dwellings were those nearest the edge where the accumulation of rubbish and sewerage had solidified over time. Rents and prices were cheaper the further out into the water. Huts cobbled together with corrugated iron and beaten tins were divided by planks no more than a foot wide so the inhabitants had to walk sideways to get about. Apparently one of the local staff in the Bank lived here but I never discovered who it was. The gulf between me and these people was truly formidable and it was as I gazed upon this forlorn sight that I began to feel the first stirrings of a social conscience that had been denied me through the narrowness of my privileged background and education. I had finally understood what true poverty really was: to own nothing in this world and to be so hungry that the last meal was a distant memory. The residents of the lagoon had probably heard a hundred times over from the priest in charge of the lean-to shelter that doubled up as a church at weekends that The Good Lord would provide, but there was no evidence of His having passed anywhere near where they lived.

The only people that could help these slum dwellers when they fell ill or needed support were local witchdoctors (as I initially called them) who resorted to age-old methods brought from Africa by the original slaves. There was a great deal of evidence of such practices on the city streets which now began to command more of my attention.

Street offering, Salvador.

Quite common was a food offering with candles and matches at the base of a tree. At a cross roads with busy traffic roaring past there was invariably an offering of some sort.

My maid Valdete once came to me in some distress saying she had seen that morning just by my front door a dead chicken and broken candles. The evil force had to be countered by some other magic. Could I let her have some more money so she could buy the necessary services from a witchdoctor? She thought someone might be jealous of our carefree lifestyle or, failing that, strictly disapproved of Rodney's nocturnal goings on with dubious ladies of the night. She only calmed down when she could assure me she had done what was required to assuage whatever it was that threatened us. There was a strange logic in all this: two equal forces, one good, the other evil; one able to dominate the other if special measures weren't taken.

Something else struck me as odd. The only people that used the smart lifts were the owners or tenants of the flats. The maids came and went in a service lift that operated in a different part of the building and they would never have used our lifts. Who was it then who had deposited the dead chicken on my doorstep? Valdete confirmed that no maid would risk being seen in a smart lift for she might well lose her job, so this meant that a fellow flat dweller, who by definition was a high earner, had gone to the trouble of leaving this potent symbol of disapproval at my door. Such practices therefore were not necessarily restricted to the poor and down-and-out.

Clearly there was a lot out there I knew nothing about. I took to visiting the *Modêlo* market down by the port during my lunch breaks where I had already noticed stalls piled high with herbs and other remedies. On closer inspection there were piles of dried herbs for curing all manner of ailments, ground rhino horn (for sexual prowess), fish scales the size of beer mats (for beauty), small metal statues of the devil complete with horns, trident and sexual apparatus (a revered and powerful god linked to the very moment of creation), tiny rag dolls (for sticking pins into and tearing off limbs), bottles of cheap perfume (a pleasant smell which, like incense, was no doubt to attract good forces), black and white powder, amulets, small bags filled with herbs to be worn round the neck. The list was endless.

One stall had a colour picture of the Christian Saint Barbara breaking out of the medieval stone tower where she was imprisoned. I saw a woman fall into a trance state as soon as she saw this picture and begin to sway wildly back and forth. But this was no Christian moment of ecstasy. Bystanders gathered round chanting in Yoruba (as I was to discover later), helping her regain her balance and fetching her a stool.

I had never seen anyone in a trance before. I knew that in some branches of the Evangelical Christian church pastors and priests conducted healing sessions among the faithful which sometimes resulted in the patient having 'a moment of ecstasy', and that throughout the Christian church during an exorcism ritual the person possessed might writhe in agony on the floor as the priest exhorted the devil to leave. I had seen photographs of Bernini's *St. Theresa In Ecstasy* (one of the Spanish mystical poets I had studied) and, like all the other teenage boys in my class, concluded that Bernini was portraying not so much a religious moment of ecstasy but an orgasmic and climactic swoon. It never occurred to me then that the two might be one and the same. Certainly the woman in trance in the market had a similar facial expression of sensual and spiritual joy. What was I witnessing and why had this woman fallen into a trance state on the chance sighting of a picture of Saint Barbara? I learned later that St. Barbara had just (1969) been removed from the liturgical calendar by Pope Paul VI because of significant doubts about her historicity but this needn't be at all pertinent for there are plenty of saints with obscure origins, not least St. George, the patron of England.

It was over a year before I fully understood what was going on, that there was a complex pantheon of Yoruba deities brought by the slaves from Africa who fitted neatly into the Christian community of saints, each god or saint a patron of some activity, or a protector against specific illnesses. Saint Barbara, the patroness of thunderbolts had, by some curious twisted logic, come to be associated with the Fire Brigade. Her Yoruba equivalent brandished an axe and fought her way through difficulties. Such a god, entering a medium, was a force to be reckoned with, a force that had the power to give hope where previously there was none. As far as the woman medium in the market was concerned, there appeared to be no difference between the third century Christian saint in the picture breaking free from her prison, and her Yoruba counterpart, swinging a double-headed axe and wearing a costume in bright fire-brigade red.

The fresh-faced youth that had stepped out of the 'plane six months earlier into the clammy Salvador air was now a young adult in a world that previously he could never have imagined really existed: a seedy world where paper-thin layers of respectability covered a person's true nature; where a man was shot dead for other men's honour; where a transvestite paraded at carnival, painted his nails and worked in a Bank; a world where fathers urged their sons to throw stones at animals; where the poor died on pavements and were pitch-forked out of sight; a strange and exciting world where primitive Indians discovered ice-cream, lone horsemen thought cars ate hay, and women in markets fell into trances. I knew that the next six months in Curitiba, some 2000 kilometres away in the far south, would be a let-down in comparison and that, from the moment I left Bahia something deep down inside me would begin to engineer my return. In my mind the Bank's days were numbered. I would continue earning my fat salary, remitting a substantial sum in hard currency every month, suffering the tedium of spending my best years slowly, like a snail, advancing towards a promotion I didn't want that promised yet more money but zero satisfaction. And then I would hand in my notice, and then..., and then...?

5

Curitiba

It was smaller and ethnically not as exciting as Salvador. I immediately missed the sticky tropical weather, the broad *Bahiano* smile, the swagger, the music and sense of style. No magical herbs here, no proximity to Africa, no local colour, no coastline, and nothing much to appeal to the senses. If you squeezed the continents together, Salvador fitted cosily beneath the projection of West Africa sharing the climate and much of the flora and fauna. But Curitiba was inland, 3000 feet up, populated mainly by Poles, Ukrainians and Germans who had each brought a measure of north European severity to bear on the city. There were Japanese too who controlled the market gardening and washed all traces of earth from vegetables before selling them. It was a sprawl of wide, sensible streets and featureless squares crammed full of traffic. Bars and restaurants tended to be inside hotels which attracted a softly-spoken middle class clientele who drank tea and fruit juice and ate cake. Street café culture was thin and invited criticism if ever anyone was so bold as to laugh. There was one lively area in the centre where young men would meet on Friday and Saturday evenings, smoke, strut the stage, rev up their motorbikes and try to attract the girls, but it was all very demure and well behaved.

The Cracovia bar, before we discovered it, was one such respectable establishment owned by Polish immigrants who had converted a ground floor room of their house to look as much as possible like the real thing back home. The walls were of exposed stone, the furniture dark and heavy, the clientele, mainly Poles and other northern European immigrants, quietly intent on drinking. We went there at weekends and virtually took the place over. Regular customers would shift positions to allow us to sit together and sing our vast repertoire of rugby songs more lustily. They sat silently with the flicker of a smile on their faces as the Polish owners energetically came and went with drinks, while we got louder and louder. Today I cringe at the thought that they might have had whole evenings ruined by our raucous behaviour but I also sometimes dare to think that on the whole our songs were enjoyed, and our boldness in singing them in public was such an unusual event in Curitiba that we were regarded with a certain degree of awe. It was as well we were the only ones who understood the crude lyrics that strictly should never have strayed from the rugby changing room, but the melodies were good and after a while I believe the odd Polish foot tapped in unison while torsos moved from side to side with the beat. Evenings ended when we got to the last song and nodded our farewells to our heavy-drinking audience. I remember a crude rustic metal door knocker on the front door which came away late one night in my hand and ended up in our flat.

Just beyond the centre along a bare street with no buildings down either side were about twenty large caravans and mobile homes, each parked permanently and each with its own power supply. This was *Frangolândia* which translates neatly into English as Chickenville, where fried chicken and chips were available throughout the day and night. Some had English names: Quick Chick (pronounced locally, *Kwi Ki Cheeky*), and Quick Dog (*Kwi Ki Doggy*) that also did a line in hotdogs. Maids from opulent houses in the suburbs queued here for the family lunch and dinner take-aways. Some of the larger mobile homes had glitzy dining rooms lit with bright neon where whole families could sit down and eat. Knives and forks were of the thinnest metal which bent as soon as they touched the food and it was impossible to find a fork that had not been twisted into fantastic shapes by idle fingers.

Beyond *Frangolândia*, standing alone in a residential street, was the ambitiously-named *Palácio* steak restaurant which in its own way had a good deal of class. The walls were covered in white tiles right up to the ceiling and each table had a sheet of paper on it for a cloth. The kitchen, from which always emerged a loud din, was behind a counter. There were only three items on the menu, steak, chips and fried onions, but once you were well known you could order your meal across a crowded room by simple hand gestures. One raised finger meant a steak, and the same finger twirled twice over secured a pile of chips and a dollop of onions. No wine list. In fact, not even water, just beer. Again, the left hand palm down and the right just above it followed by the requisite number of fingers communicated to the waiter across the hubbub of the room precisely how many beers you wanted to order. The smell of the fried onions got into your clothes and stayed with you for hours.

There was one very posh restaurant, always empty, called the *Ile de France* which had a blue, white and red neon Eiffel Tower flashing in the window. Here there was starched linen and a very correct French lady who offered French wine at fabulous prices without recommending anything else. The new Brazilian vineyards were still very much in their infancy with some grand-sounding names such as *Château Duvallier* (Bordeaux style), *Santa Ursula* (the name means 'little female bear' in Latin and the wine was suitably precocious) and a high alcohol dry white appropriately called *Navio Sem Rumo* ('Ship without a course'). None of them tasted like the French equivalent but prices were fair, and in the cooler climate of Curitiba it was refreshing to have a change from beer.

A few gracious buildings had survived but in the main the half dozen or so high rise blocks in the centre were not memorable and larger buildings such as the Post Office, a singularly ugly concrete building of the late 1950s in curiously Soviet style, were very soon overtaken by simple single storey dwellings as you walked away from the centre. The year I arrived (1969) the city council, under the leadership of Mayor Omar Sabbag and architect and urban planner Jaime Lerner, both now local heroes, embarked on a highly ambitious programme of urban planning and public transport. The city has since won numerous prizes for its ecological innovations and is often described as 'the most American' of Brazil's cities, which I cynically regard as a somewhat dubious accolade. There was not much in 1969 to suggest that the Town Hall was a hive of creative thought but we were almost certainly living through a period of enforced stagnation before the bulldozers moved in. Today there is no doubt: Curitiba is now regarded the world over as a shining example of how urban planners can get things right. In 1969 there was no indication to people living there that such a transformation was about to take place.

The State of Paraná of which Curitiba is the capital gives its name to the parana pine tree, and the word Curitiba means 'much pine' in the local *Guaraní* toponymy. Shiploads of dressed timber were trucked from the forests to the sea port of Paranaguá, some two hours down the road, destined for the European building and furniture markets. In the past the Bank had financed coffee exports all over the world but the coffee glut had hit Brazil badly and there were now numerous warehouses piled high with seven or eight year old coffee that took a long time to shift and that the Bank was unwilling to accept as a guarantee. So export business hardly boomed. Even the local staff found it difficult to occupy their day fully and we trainees were hard put to find anything useful or stimulating to do.

The clerk who ran the foreign exchange desk was one-armed and needed physical assistance every time he added a note to his book. He could write well enough with his good hand but needed someone else (invariably the trainee sitting by his side) to hold the ruler whilst he drew a pencil line. This was the sum total of excitement during the course of many a humdrum day. The manager, in despair at our enforced idleness, kept dreaming up things to keep us occupied. For some obscure reason he thought it important to inform Head Office in London how many miles the Bank's two official cars did to the gallon, so I had to convert litres and kilometres to gallons and miles. I was also ordered to make a plan of the Bank's two floors for Head Office which I did happily enough converting with my atrocious mathematics the metres on the Bank's tape measure into yards, feet and inches. All went swimmingly until, to my utter consternation, I discovered that the first floor was considerably larger than the ground floor. The local staff laughed out loud when they saw this over-paid trainee leave the building, cross the street and gaze in uncomprehending disbelief at the first floor that, yes, fitted snugly on top of the ground floor, so why wasn't it the same size? On another occasion I was sent into the country to verify the assets of a stud farm and in my report, again for London, I found I had written in true Dixon of Dock Green style the immortal words: 'A bull was sighted'. I never found out whether or not these communications went any further than the London mail clerk who opened the envelopes but nobody ever questioned my calculations or my observations.

Rosie had now finished her degree with considerable distinction and was preparing to come and join me. Her last letter before leaving confirmed that she had managed to do all the idiosyncratic shopping I had requested:

Horsham, W. Sussex, 23 July 1969

...In the end I had to go to Old Bond Street for your pipes. I got a very handsome meerschaum calabash in the style of Sherlock Holmes, and a Churchwarden that is over a foot long, just like the

clay you gave me but made of briar so no danger of snapping. I'm also bringing a couple of tins of Balkan Sobranie (white top with black lettering) as a special treat...

Arrangements as ever were tiresomely difficult as letters sometimes took up to three weeks to arrive and even telegrams were unreliable because at the weekends they piled up at the Post Office and were only delivered on Monday morning. I would probably not learn if her flight was to be cancelled at the last minute, or delayed some hours. I had managed to get her a job teaching English at the British Council English School in Curitiba by writing very formally to the Head mentioning her first class Modern Languages degree from Cambridge. His reply was swift and direct; 'Of course there's no need for me to see her beforehand. There aren't many Cambridge Firsts in the whole of Brazil, let alone Curitiba'. I went to the *Ile de France* restaurant, reserved the best table and told Madame to pull out all the stops as I would be in the company of my future wife who, among her many other attributes (one of which was to smoke clay churchwarden pipes), was a very fine cook. But of course in my excitement I forgot she might be exhausted, physically as well as emotionally, after a long haul flight with a refuelling stop at Recife, changing airports at São Paulo in the rush hour, and catching a small turbo-prop that bumped and wheezed all the way to Curitiba. By the time we were finally reunited all she wanted was a cold drink and a long sleep but we stuck to the dinner plan, toyed with over-rich food, and much to Madame's disappointment, left early.

Life for me began to look up. Rosie discovered the vegetable markets that were run by Japanese immigrants who washed and polished every tomato and turnip till they shone and looked irresistible. We ate like kings in our flat above the Bank and had a maid called Maria Juana whom we called Hash (but not to her face) and who thought I looked like a waiter in my tuxedo on the evening when, with nothing better to do, we decided to dress for dinner. Every day I lazily came and went to the Bank by lift and soon developed a habit of popping back for a snack or cold drink without anyone questioning my absence.

With the eyes of a newcomer Rosie noticed things that had passed me by. Pretty well everything apart from food and drink could be bought on the Never Never: jewellery, electrical goods, and all items of clothing including underwear. The price displayed was not the full purchase price but simply one of ten or twenty monthly payments, so at first sight everything in the shops seemed inordinately cheap. When you asked the hapless assistant for the full purchase price you had to wait some minutes while the calculation was made at the back of the shop.

The weekend we spent at Iguaçú Falls on the border between Brazil, Argentina and Paraguay inspired a long letter home from Rosie with occasional, perfectly justifiable, lapses into purplish prose:

Curitiba, 27th August 1969

...The Falls are magnificent. You round a bend in the road and then suddenly, there they are. And not just one fall, but dozens of little ones, cascades pouring out of what seem to be little holes in the jungle on the Argentine side, tumbling over rocks

in a long succession with tranquil little pools in between where you can take out a boat and fish or swim. It was a perfect day for photos, very hot and sunny, and there were some interesting colours because the rivers have been so full in the last few weeks with all the rain (there have been some quite serious floods in the valleys) that torrents of rust-coloured muddy water were pouring over catching the sun. I really cannot find words to describe it adequately. The water trickling slowly over the top of the escarpment and gathering momentum on the way down looked like melted sugar, just beginning to turn into caramel, the same consistency and the same pale golden brown colour at the top of the rocks in the sun. The description sounds very mundane but it's the only way I can think of to give you an idea of the colour. Then there are the big cascades like the 'Devil's Throat', where the water is already moving fast when it reaches the sheer face and then pours over with the solidity and energy of a human body. It reminded me of an athlete or an acrobat (perhaps because of the colour too) turning and turning his body in continual somersaults, full of controlled energy. We were able to get terrifyingly close to the edge of the fall and have taken some splendid photos on the very edge of one of the biggest cataracts. The place was thick with Yanks all cine filming everything like mad and cooing with delight. We wondered down little paths to the foot of one of the largest falls where there is an elevator up to the road for weary middle-aged Connecticut legs which we of course didn't take. We walked along a ramshackle-looking bridge built out over the top of the next fall which so far only goes half way and so looks all the more perilous as it ends in mid stream. Walking along it you get soaked to the skin with spray. Screams of ecstatic horror from the Minnesota Ladies' Club.

Paul slept like a baby all the way back to Curitiba in the bus (seven hours). I can't say I was so fortunate. For some inexplicable reason, in this tropical country, bus seats are invariably covered in plastic. Very sticky...

We became friendly with Christopher from the British Council who imported a brand new shining soft-top Triumph from England in which we went down to the coast singing and waving our arms wildly with wind in our hair in search of barbecued fish and ice cold beer served under palm awnings on the beach. But it wasn't the same as Salvador and there was nothing apart from fresh pineapple and ice cream. The next time we filled the car with food and beer, built our own fire in a hole in the sand, cooked the chicken too fast and spent an uncomfortable night in a wooden chalet with a creaking veranda on sheets covered in fine white sand with no running water and mosquitoes whining overhead.

The narrow road to the sea port of Paranaguá wound its way from the 3000 foot plateau where Curitiba sprawled along its main arteries, down through dark and impenetrable forests, past ruined houses and the occasional petrol station with stalls outside selling chilled drinks. Occasionally we would stop the car to allow an enormous iguana, at least a metre long, to shamble across the road, its spiked head and back glinting with a myriad of colours, dragging a torso and tail with folds and sags in the skin like a worn, over-sized suit. None of us dared to get too close in case the tongue shot out and covered us in glue. Apparently they are delicious to eat although we never saw them on a restaurant menu. The flora and fauna changed dramatically as we lost height and went through zones of different coloured flowers and butterflies before arriving at thick forest at sea level with stout Tarzan-style lianas growing down from the tallest trees. Like children we swung out over the road (mercifully not very fast or busy in those days), our thick dark hair catching the wind, whooping and beating chests.

Curitiba, 4th September 1969

... We turned off the main highway on to a beaten earth road with a very smooth surface that was a lot better to drive on than any of the asphalted roads but with many notices expressly prohibiting the use of the road in case of rain. It was very hot indeed with that damp jungle atmosphere pervading everything. We recorded some of the bird noises and other sounds of insect life with which the place was alive. It's fantastic to be able to look up and see all sorts of multi-coloured parrots squawking around

No cars in the event of rain.

above you, and lush orchids of every shade of purple and red peeping out of the parasitic liana halfway up trees. There were a lot of dead leaves and branches all over the floor and I suddenly noticed one of these leaves jump. We looked more closely and saw that it was a horned toad, about six inches long, perfectly camouflaged and exactly the same colour as the leaves. We then pushed on and the further away we got from civilisation the more primitive the huts became, until the little wooden huts with tiled and corrugated iron roofs that are just outside Curitiba began to seem quite luxurious in comparison with the loosely constructed log huts with roofs of cut branches and dried leaves, and naked or scantily dressed children peeping inquisitively out of the doors as we went past. There was a card pinned on a wall signed by the anti-malaria team, who come round to all these outlying huts at intervals and spray the whole place. A man told us that there was quite a lot of malaria round there, and this was borne out by people in Curitiba when we got back so we resolved that next time we would go well armed with anti-malaria pills, and also a syringe and anti-snake serum, just in case...

Paranaguá itself was pretty dead with just the small port showing any sign of life but the narrow side streets with single storey buildings each with its faded shutters and front door visible behind clusters of electric wires could have been lifted from a Portuguese village years previously and transported here intact. The biggest attraction were the beaches: great stretches of white sand with absolutely no-one there but us, not even a palm-roofed bar with cold drinks, and great Atlantic rollers roaring and sucking after their long journey from the west coast of Africa. I lost my father's ring off my finger attempting to jump a roller, scrabbling around beneath it trying to regain my balance. But the soapy water had taken it and the swirling sand hid it from our sight as we tried in vain to find a gleam of gold among the restless rush of pebbles. Someone will have it now with its tiny inset diamond glinting for attention like a piercing on a lip, all its family history snatched from it, while I still have in the pit of my stomach that sense of loss. I see it on his hand darting up and down the keyboard every night at my bedtime, magically transforming ivory and black into the silky notes of a Chopin prelude and then holding my head for a kiss.

Curitiba, 18th September 1969

...This time on our way back we stopped at a tiny village called Tagaçaba by a wide river only about 15 kms from the sea.

Tagaçaba villagers. 'Ah, Inglaterra, maravilhas'.

We drove down a dirt track to some huts where we found a family sitting on the ground outside in front of an impressive pile of fresh-caught fish which they were gutting, all working together at different jobs like a human conveyor belt. The two men rushed off as soon as they saw us coming and then emerged slowly and rather diffidently buttoning up their Sunday best shirts donned specially for the visitors. They were friendly and we got talking, Paul recording the whole thing on tape. They were amazed to hear that we came from England, though I was quite surprised to find that one of the men had heard of it and knew it lay to the east.

'Ah', he said, 'Inglaterra, maravilhas'.

It must be some kind of far-off fairy land to them. He talked for some time about the lot of the poor and how many men he knew in the village who had never once left it. He was the only one, so he said proudly, who had been to Curitiba, and that was a long way off. He talked of São Paulo as the stepping stone to the world with its vast roads leading in and out of the city and said that once you got as far as São Paulo you could get to the 'fim do mundo', to the ends of the earth. At this stage we played back some of the recording. You can imagine their faces. They were all quite spellbound, taking in every word. Just as we were leaving the other man said:

'You know, I had a dream last night and in this dream a very beautiful Senhora came from São Paulo bringing fine new things for my farm, and she had blue eyes and curly hair and was dressed in good quality material. It just goes to show, dreams do sometimes come true. And if you can't dream, you've got nothing. Dreams are so important in life.'

Whereupon everyone agreed and said that at least if the

fine new things weren't at the farm in the morning he had got the blue-eyed Senhora from São Paulo. Our car, registered in São Paulo, added veracity to the story.

Back on the highway we found a black and yellow snake in the middle of the road that had been stunned by a passing car. It was still very much alive but we put a safe end to it and brought it back home and it is now gracing the sitting room of our flat in a bottle of alcohol. It's incredibly beautiful but one of the clerks in the Bank has told us it has a vicious bite and that next time we should stand well clear.

Someone persuaded me to spend a Saturday morning in a vintage cream and red two-seater 'plane with an instructor so that I could experience looping the loop. I had been talked through what it would feel like but nothing can prepare you for the suddenness of every ounce of your body weight rushing from your head down to your feet, and the frightening convex picture of Curitiba directly above the cockpit which you see through bulging eyes. The 'plane was terrifying enough: manufactured in 1930, one engine, open cockpit and a single parachute that was worn, not by the inexperienced passenger, but by the instructor. Two controls: a yard-long joystick that seemed loose and ineffectual to the touch, and an altimeter that revealed Curitiba's high altitude before we took off.

Rosie stood to one side of the corrugated hanger as we taxied towards the grass runway, convinced she would never see me again. I was too intent on strapping myself in (thank God they hadn't skimped on the straps) and attaching a soft leather Bomber Command helmet with goggles to think that something might go wrong. The acrid burning exhaust,

Preparing to loop the loop.

sputtering engine and creaking worn coachwork as we bumped along the stretch of grass at, surely, far too low a speed to take off, filled me with utter fear, though I daren't show it because the instructor, a Japanese with a blood red pullover and no Portuguese, kept an eye on me through a mirror. I need hardly have worried about not being able to speak to him. When we finally got up in the air the din and shuddering were so frightful that I couldn't have heard a word anyway. We looped the loop, and then, just as the lead-weight began to ooze back towards my centre of gravity, we looped the loop again. Thumbs up through the mirror from the Japanese instructor; distinct thumbs down from me although it took me some seconds to get my fingers to work. It was minutes before I could get my legs back and make my way gingerly out of the 'plane. They promised there was no better cure for a lingering hang-over, and they were right.

The days passed slowly and sometimes the aching boredom of the Bank and the dreadful sense that I was growing old sending other people's telegrams and drawing lines in ledgers got the better of me and I would go to the flat, slam doors and punch my pillow. At least in Salvador when the going got depressingly dull in the Bank, there were many things to do and wonder at outside. But here in Curitiba where the northern European influence was strong there was nothing much in the centre that we found endearing and yet every day we needed the stimulus of change from the Bank's monotonous routine. I had been away from England for almost a year getting well paid for doing a job that wasn't a job at all. I longed to be stretched, to be given just an ounce of responsibility, but above all I longed to be involved with something that was worthwhile. Measuring rooms in centimetres then converting my measurements into feet and inches was just the sort of thing I used to do for Maths homework at Prep. School. Although I still hadn't mastered the skill of such conversions I thought I was capable of a lot more than that.

Christmas loomed and we needed cheering up. Somehow, after a long 'chat' on the Telex machine, I managed to persuade the staff manager to invite me to spend a day in São Paulo to discuss how I was developing as a trainee. I had a great deal to tell him about wasted opportunities and thumb twiddling but he allowed me only fifteen minutes (how can you possibly justify a long 'plane journey for a mere fifteen minutes-worth of chat?) during which he did all the talking, informing me in minute fourteen that I was being transferred after Christmas to Fortaleza. All my plans to let off steam and lecture him on how to run a trainee course successfully were scuppered at a stroke, but at least the shortness of my meeting left me hours of time to do a lot of shopping before my return flight. A bright and sympathetic-looking secretary (not the sort we had in the Bank in Curitiba) was able to direct me to a shop where I might find English delicacies and fill an empty suitcase. They had mince meat, Christmas puddings, crackers with silly jokes, and tinned Camembert cheese from France with a notice just inside the lid saying 'Cheese connoisseurs will be aware that this cheese is supposed to smell bad'.

6

Fortaleza

Fortaleza, capital of Ceará, further north than Salvador, and on the coast, earns just half a page in *The South American Handbook*. Compare this with Salvador's two and a half pages that have been written by a man who clearly fell in love with everything he saw. He had no such love affair when he got to Fortaleza for what the reader learns about the city and surrounding district is hardly an incitement to visit: 'It has a protected roadstead where ships drawing up to 27 feet discharge into lighters at Mucuripe Point, 5 miles east of the town. There is an unfinished quay wall 930 metres long for ships drawing 14 to 21 feet...There are fair motor tracks throughout the state of Ceará and there are roads to Recife, Rio de Janeiro (now being paved), and Brasília.' By far the longest entry in the *Handbook* is the list of Banks, fifteen of them, but why Fortaleza needed so many different Banks was always a mystery. The *Handbook* makes no mention of anything worthwhile in the city for the very good reason that at the time there was nothing of any architectural or historical merit. Indeed, it was a city of half a million people with no recognisable centre although there was a single street lined with shops selling gaudy man-made fabrics, polythene tubs and boxes, and cheap household goods.

Nowadays the 'plane takes some minutes to fly over the hundreds of towering high rise blocks as it comes in to land, but when we went there in early 1970 the tallest buildings were the shell of the unfinished cathedral and a new four storey hotel with a glass door on to a foyer painted in dark terracotta that was regarded with some awe by the local people. On the top floor was an expensive bar with classy furniture and wide views over cluttered roofscapes, and the barman sighed wistfully as we ordered drinks and cashew nuts worth more than he would earn in a week. He was an accurate reflection of what was happening outside. Behind the neon lights and glitter of the nearby shops lurked a good measure of depression. Each shop employed an assistant in a tight suit with a permanent crease ironed on the jacket sleeves to stand on the pavement and attract passers-by. First a hiss to get attention, then a loud and urgent '*Ô freguês!*' ('Hey, you, customer!') followed by sales patter: 'In here for the best cloth...Try on these shoes'. Being taller than most and white-skinned we stood out as foreigners who were an easy catch so whole streets would hiss and jostle in an attempt to secure our custom.

The unfinished cathedral, the third largest church in the country, loomed eerily in a square and attracted attention because of its huge bulk. Every time money earmarked for the cathedral's construction ran short the city council commissioned and chose different architectural plans so the building was a hotchpotch of styles, the lower section of the walls of course being of the earliest design. Many windows were empty holes through which pigeons came and went, and the downward slope of the floor from the altar to the west door had quickly caught on as an ideal location for lorries to change their oil so there was a steady stream of motorised traffic up and down the aisle, a permanent stench of diesel fuel and a long viscous oil slick. A French friend unkindly referred to it as a ruin still being constructed in the Romanesque style, but despite all the considerable logistical problems it was in regular use for services and weddings. Fortunately for brides with full length white gowns and trains there was a plastic mat that was unrolled at the altar and stretched the length of the aisle. Photographs outside had piles of rubble, skips, cranes and building materials as their backcloth.

Letter to the Editor, *The South American Handbook,* dated February 10th, 1970:

Dear Sir,

You mention on page 20 of the latest 1964 edition of your esteemed publication that 'in many tropical places there is a marked difference in temperature between the interior of cathedrals and the outer air.' You go on to point out that the problem is more marked at higher altitudes where 'the danger of pulmonary disease is greater'. However, I feel you should point out in future editions of the Handbook *that the majority of the windows of the cathedral at Fortaleza (N.E. Brazil) are unglazed and that the West 'Door' does not yet have a door so remains open throughout the day and night. As a result, the interior temperature is always the same as the outside temperature. Travellers can visit, sure in the knowledge that colds cannot be contracted here and that there is no danger of pulmonary disease. Building work, always very slow, comes to a halt every few months so this situation is likely to pertain for a considerable time to come.*

Yours faithfully etc.

Our house was on the outskirts of town quite close to a slum from which emerged a regular number of would-be thieves who came and rattled our windows late at night. The windows had no glass, just open wooden slats and we often saw the thief's fingers inside our room trying to find the catch. Soon these would-be thieves had to share all their ill-gotten gains with hordes of starving people from the interior converging on the city in search of food since their own crops had failed, burned to a crisp in the relentless sun. They came to be known as *os flagelados* (literally, the flagellated ones), a new word that crept in to the vocabulary to describe the appalling situation in which they found themselves. 1970 was a year of such unremitting drought that a state of emergency had to be declared in Ceará and this resulted in basic foodstuffs being brought to the city on lorries to cope with the ever-increasing demand. There was no variety: black beans, rice, *farofa* (manioc flour) and carrots were the staples. The better off could buy chicken but there was very little else. Fishermen off the coast might have done a very good trade at this time but the newcomers had no money and those that did not resort to crime were forced to beg. One evening as we sat on the terrace of a bar overlooking waves breaking on pure white sand just a few metres from us, we were approached by some thirty people over the course of the evening desperate for food. The waiter tried in vain to keep them out but there were too many. One man with a child in his arms pushed him out of the way shouting: 'I am hungry. I have to eat. So does my child. You *have* to let me in'.

The baker's shop a few metres down the street from our house never had any bread at times when we wanted it but pride stopped them from admitting it. So the conversation went like this:

'Have you any bread?'

'Yes, plenty...but none just now'.

This response always made the baker and his customer laugh but there was nothing remotely amusing about it. There simply wasn't enough flour available for the bakery to provide loaves even for people who could afford it because flour was not regularly included as a staple brought to the city on the food lorries. The lot of the very poor was dire for they had to rely exclusively on charity and, since there were so many of them, there was a limit to how much the more prosperous were prepared to help.

Butch Cassidy and the Sundance Kid was showing in all the cinemas at the time and the catchy theme music with its poignant lyrics about ceaseless rain could be heard in bars and restaurants, and wafted out of windows all over town. The desperately poor can't have understood the lyrics as they begged from table to table but the students who were mainly from more secure backgrounds swayed in time to the music mouthing the words into fake microphones and shouting at barmen if they dared change the track:

Raindrops keep fallin' on my head.
But that doesn't mean my eyes will soon be turnin' red.
Cryin's not for me,
'Cause I'm never gonna stop the rain by complainin'
Because I'm free,
Nothin's worryin' me.

In fact, two distinct things were worrying me at this time: my eyes were playing tricks and I could feel with my tongue the sharp edges of a cavity in one of my teeth. The thought of placing myself in the hands of an optician and a dentist in this depressed corner of northeast Brazil filled me with alarm so I lived for a few weeks with the notion that all might be well until my return to England. But this was wishful thinking.

The harsh neon lights in the Bank cast their cold light in to the darkest corners with a virtually imperceptible flicker which I readily perceived when I narrowed my eyes and concentrated on the objects on my desk. The flickering then became very hard to live with and only diminished if I opened my eyes wide and stared at people or objects on the other side of the room. Naturally this had to be done with a certain degree of circumspection and once or twice I caught the bemused gaze of a colleague who clearly felt unnerved by my gawping at him wide-eyed in an attempt to regain focus and banish the awful flickering. Local staff were used to bored, over-indulged English trainees with nothing to do but this must have taken the biscuit. When I mentioned the flickering to Milton, the oddly-named Bank factotum who came round twice a day with coffee, he said that other trainees had complained about precisely the same thing and he had always sent them to an optician's just round the corner. I decided to risk it. After all, an eye test should be nothing to worry about.

'Ah, the flickering neon', said the optician as soon as I explained what was wrong, 'have they still done nothing about it? I can make some spectacles for you that should do the trick'.

Most of the frames on display from which I should make my choice were tawdry and unbecoming with adjustable wire arms that clung to the back of the ear. I selected a pair of gold half-moons which I thought would sit well on the tip of my nose and give the impression that I only suffered from slight myopia, but when they were ready the lenses had a pronounced sickly green hue that communicated 'Blind man approaching; make way fast'. The optician, whose degree certificate sat framed in the window, assured me the green would stop the flickering and that he had 'cured' many others in the same way. The glasses were a hit with my colleagues in the Bank who all wanted to try them on, pushing them to the top of their nose then strutting around with their head thrown back at an angle shouting 'Sherlock Holmes' (pronounced 'Sherlock-ee Ol-mees'). At one point the Accountant, an officious little man whom I sensed disliked me, ran up the stairs to our floor to ascertain what on earth was going on. With pronounced sense of humour deficiency he commanded us all to get back to work throwing a glance in my direction to indicate that I really should know better. This little altercation was to develop later into a major crisis that almost ended in my getting the sack but at the time I dismissed it as one of those unfortunate things that temporarily tarnish the relationship between a lowly trainee and his immediate superior.

I went to the dentist on April 21st and immediately regretted it. The surgery was on the first floor of a crumbling building so there was no chance of sneaking a look through a window before taking the plunge. I rang the bell and the door was opened by the dentist himself who, on shaking my hand, smiled broadly and revealed a set of far from impeccable teeth glinting dully in a mouth surrounded by untidy stubble. This shattered my already faltering confidence because at that time an unshaven chin was not the fashion accessory that it has since become. A stubbly dentist to my mind was a man who paid scant attention to detail but now, with the door firmly shut behind me, I was entrapped and unable to extricate myself. I noticed with some alarm that all the windows were permanently blacked out, there was no fresh air and the whole surgery was lit by bright, slightly flickering neon. With my green half-moon spectacles firmly on my nose I sank in to the worn leatherette chair and felt the prickles of horsehair from the bald armrests through my shirt sleeves. An electric fan hummed somewhere behind me.

'Today is Tiradentes Day and I should be on holiday', he said re-arranging his fearsome instruments in a chipped white enamel bowl. 'You are familiar with Tiradentes I trust?'

It is difficult to spend longer than a few days in Brazil without gleaning that Tiradentes is a national hero of considerable renown. There are statues of him in all the big cities and countless streets, squares, hospitals and schools are named after him. His plan was to declare Brazil a Republic but the authorities got to him first, subjected him to a trial that lasted nearly three years, hanged and quartered him in Rio de

Janeiro, then wrote a document in his own blood denouncing him. He had at one stage worked as a dentist hence the nickname Tiradentes which translates neatly in to English as 'Tooth-puller'.

My own tooth-puller recounted his version of this to me as he poked and probed inside my mouth, breathing stale breath in to my face and stopping occasionally to polish the steam off his thick convex glasses. In my immediate field of vision were his stained teeth surrounded by stubble, and above and around him a fantastic selection of chromium pulleys joined by black rubber bands. This was the business end of an aged electric drilling machine that whirred and whined for ten to fifteen seconds at a time then emitted a noise of grinding metal at which point the tooth-puller swore, removed the instrument from my mouth, knelt down by the chair to re-thread a pulley and then, tutting with indignation, started all over again. This was hardly a work routine designed to put a nervous patient at his ease. The tooth-puller could not stretch to any anaesthetic so the pain and discomfort were considerable.

When the gold crown arrived after a few days he assured me it would take two minutes to fix but his impression was faulty and so was the crown so he ground my tooth further and re-shaped the crown with a file, carefully collecting the filings in a napkin. When I queried his astronomical fee he reduced it by twenty five per cent. I subsequently checked the *South American Handbook* but there wasn't a single reference to dental care throughout the whole country. The crown has since been superseded by modern and painless root canal treatment but I still have the crown in a stud box and the crude scars from the filing are quite plain to the naked eye.

The whole unpleasant experience with the dentist as recounted here soon palled to insignificance when compared with what was shortly to befall me. I was imprisoned every day in an upper room lit by borrowed light from a large internal window overlooking the ground floor of the Bank. An idle man raising his eyes to our window would see me at my desk on one side of the room and half a dozen secretaries opposite me in a typing pool, each vying with the other for the longest finger nails painted in bright enamel. There was one amusing moment when they all screeched and jumped on to their desks like over-active cartoon characters. When I asked them what on earth was the matter they all pointed a gaudy talon at a black furry ball behind the telephone on my desk. How a tarantula had managed to get into the Bank, up a flight of stairs and on to my desk I have no idea, but it certainly knew how to make its presence felt. Amid the panic I heard them all in unison shouting at me to ring for the porter, then they screamed uncontrollably as I reached out towards the 'phone. Didn't I know that tarantulas can travel at 30 kilometres an hour? Someone must have gone to fetch the porter because suddenly he was there creeping up on the spider, a broom in one hand and a dustpan and brush in the other.

It was all over very quickly and I had earned myself the reputation of being somewhat rash which did not stand me in good stead when, some weeks later during yet another torrid afternoon of utter boredom when I had nothing better to occupy my mind, I rang the Accountant on the internal 'phone and, very, very stupidly, thinking he would see the joke, told him that the Bank driver delivering payrolls had just been attacked. He hit the panic button and alarm bells sounded in every room. Within seconds armed police were scurrying around, automatic weapons at the ready, while I sheepishly sought to explain to the Brazilian Accountant what had really happened, but he persisted in wiping the floor with me, delighted at last to be able to speak his mind. I heard 'never' and 'again' and *vagabundo* followed by razor-sharp adjectives and remember an angrily-wagging finger very close to my face. Of course it was wrong, crying wolf and all that, and yes I realized I was risking other people's safety, and no, never again, it would never happen again. Tail firmly between my legs I returned to my desk unable to look the half a dozen typists in the face, which is just as well because I knew that each would be smirking from ear to ear.

Gods in their heaven occasionally grow bored and seek out mortals for a bit of sport. Hermes, patron of thieves and liars, lost no time. Minutes after the armed police had left with a squeal of sirens my door burst open and there, blood pouring from his brow, was the Bank driver who this time had really been ambushed on the road with £35000 in cash in a canvas bag. Piercing screams from the secretaries who, like the rest of us, still hadn't got over the horror of the armed police; loud and unprintable oath from the Accountant who slammed the 'phone down and refused to pick up the receiver again; valuable minutes lost while the police satisfied themselves that this time we were being serious. I do not know why they didn't sack me then. For weeks I expected a communication from London and crept around with lead in my heart worrying what the long-term effects would be if I were sacked, and very concerned that they might not pay my very expensive air fare back to London. But there was nothing. In fact, the Accountant gave a party on his birthday and invited all the staff including me. He got his own back though. There was a big spiky plant halfway up the garden path leading to his front door. For some reason, probably nerves, I tripped over it inflicting considerable pain and bleeding that forced me to retire early.

7

South to Rio

June, 1970, and I had been away for 18 months. Letters from home were wistful accounts of a staid and repetitive life in our roomy Victorian house which stood grandly at the bottom of a leafy drive in the heart of Surrey. There were occasional guarded comments about my cousins' love lives, the corresponding inevitable drop in moral standards, and a failing marriage. All this seemed very far away to us and not at all important, although we were sensitive enough to remember that in my family such things took on the epic dimensions of earthquakes at the top end of the Richter Scale. I had an uncle who despaired at seeing black and white pictures on the television of a man and a woman kissing, and once wrote to the BBC when he saw innocent footage of happily married couples in bed together sipping early morning tea.

When news came of my forthcoming transfer to Rio de Janeiro hints were dropped that at some stage my father might abandon the cosiness of home and come and visit for two or three weeks. Naturally we were pleased but what on earth would he do during the working day all by himself without a word of Portuguese to help him on his way? I tried to dissuade him saying that the next six months would be over quickly and that I would be home for Christmas, but somehow the idea got firmly lodged in his mind. It would be his first ever trip outside Europe; he would fly Air France from Paris direct (at least the food would be good); and would I please ensure I find a flat with a spare room. We never thought he'd take the plunge and pushed the whole matter to the backs of our minds while we focused on the utter delight of spending our last months in the *cidade maravilhosa* (city of marvels).

Our definitive journey from Fortaleza to Rio through the backlands and then down the coast for hundreds of miles was in a bus. The *leito*, or 'bed' bus was a new phenomenon in Brazil that was supposed to coincide with the surfacing of all the main roads linking the largest cities but the buses arrived some years before the tarmac so there were sections of the journey that were not as smooth as the publicity would have you believe. The *leito* when driving over tarmac lived up to its name and, as buses go, was surprisingly comfortable. It was a little like travelling first class in an aeroplane: the seat, a triumph of engineering in itself, could be extended and converted in to a flat bed which meant that each bus contained no more than about twenty passengers. There was a smartly attired hostess, two drivers, a 'fridge full of cold drinks on the house, and a tiny bathroom complete with shower right at the back.

When Milton booked our tickets, for a fraction of the cost he could have chosen seats on an ordinary bus or, for a mere pittance we could have travelled on what was commonly known as a *pau de arara*. The ordinary bus would have delivered us more or less safely to our destination but we would have had all the tiresome inconveniences of other people's picnic smells, alien heads resting on our shoulders and the relentless whingeing of over-tired children, not forgetting a whole set of twenty-year-old shock absorbers. A journey to Rio on a *pau de arara* on the other hand would have left us gibbering wrecks. We once took a short ride on one just for the experience but it was an experience we were keen not to repeat. *Pau de arara* means 'parrot perch' and, as the name implies, there are no seats. Strictly speaking there is no bus either, just an ancient lorry with wooden struts fixed from side to side over which the hapless traveller places his arms then takes the weight off his feet by literally hanging in mid air, his feet only just touching the floor of the lurching lorry. Even a short journey leaves all passengers with numbness in the upper body and vicious bruises around the armpits.

Our spanking new *leito*, however, was in an entirely different class but the frequent stops at roadside inns brought you in to contact with travellers who weren't so fortunate. The *pau de arara* lorries stopped for some hours at these places in order to permit their exhausted passengers to recover the use of their limbs and snatch a few moments' sleep so the cafeteria chairs were all taken by sprawling families, their heads resting on the table tops. Out of the bus window we saw sun-bleached wooden houses with skinny animals behind and grimy children running alongside us alarmingly close to the wheels, arms outstretched, hoping for a coin, but the air conditioning demanded hermetically sealed windows so eventually they broke away disappointed. Many of the houses stood empty with drifts of dust against the door, each with its thorn-fenced dry corral.

The exodus from the *sertão* (interior scrubland) had started in earnest with São Paulo and Rio bearing the brunt of men and women seeking a better life after years of drought and deprivation in the depressed northeast. We saw whole families, their meagre possessions in cardboard suitcases stitched in to a piece of old cloth for added protection, destined for the worst slums on the outskirts of town, still full of hope at this stage that some gainful employment would come their way. But the vast majority left a rural wilderness where even the animals died, in favour of an urban environment ruled by thugs where corruption, prostitution and drugs held sway. Middle class television soaps ignored the very grim reality of abject poverty and filled the minds of simple rural folk with glittering tales of what life in the cities was like. And so they flocked in their thousands, as if drawn by a magnet, only to discover within weeks that they had swapped one corner of Hell for another.

The long road to Rio was not entirely paved and there were whole sections with cars, lorries and buses waiting to be hauled out of the mud while we bumped along between the trees on either side avoiding the road altogether. Near the fords for crossing rivers were signs of the first footings for road bridges and we missed by a matter of weeks the completion of the ambitious project to link the northeast with the big cities of the south by paved road. We just coincided with the tail end of motorised transport as it must have been for decades.

8

Rio de Janeiro

Everyone said what a special place Rio was with dramatic islands rising out of a turquoise sea edged with miles of gleaming white sand; gracious palaces, Baroque churches and established parks; home to household names such as Sugar Loaf Mountain and Copacabana Beach. After the drab provincialism of Fortaleza and Curitiba we looked forward to a lot of sophistication and more than a little class. How disappointed we were to discover that rents along the miles of beach were astronomical (higher apparently than 5th Avenue, New York) and that dinner and drinks cost on average three times more than we were used to. But it was a one-off and we determined to make the most of it.

We settled on a pretty ground floor flat in Copacabana along Toneleiros, the street that is furthest from the beach but which offers tantalising glimpses of the jungle behind through occasional breaks in the buildings. A few yards down on the same side of the street as our building was a small shop selling a variety of goods reminiscent of the stalls in Salvador's *Modêlo* market: packets of herbs, small amulets, powders and strings of cheap metal beads interspersed with crescent moons, tridents, single and double-headed axes, swords and taut bows and arrows. Arranged on shelves from floor to ceiling was an astonishing collection of statues painted in gaudy colours. On the pavement outside stood a life-sized statue of a burly Indian in a bright green loin cloth aiming a bow and arrow at passers-by; on the threshold, a one-foot high statue of an old black man with white hair and incongruously scarlet lips squatting on his haunches.

The shop had *Caboclo - Umbanda* written large above the window. I was very ignorant about all this at the time but gleaned enough from the shopkeeper to learn that the term *caboclo* from the Indian language *Guaraní* means 'copper-coloured', which by extension describes any native Brazilian Indian. In more recent times it has been used to describe anyone of mixed race. As far as this curious shop was concerned however, it was a generic term covering the wide array of herbs, substances and statues on display aimed primarily at slum dwellers with menial jobs who bussed in to the centre every day. These people practised *umbanda*, a Yoruba term covering the various blends of African and Christian religions that have come together in Rio. The shop did a brisk trade and we often saw statues of different sizes being carried down the street on the first stage of their journey to a distant dwelling in the suburbs. I was going to have to wait for some time before seeing individual shrines in people's houses but the shopkeeper, probably expecting to sell some of her wares to a couple of interested tourists, took great pains to explain what the different statues represented: the squatting figure in the doorway was *preto velho* (old black man) representing the spirits of old slaves who died in captivity or after being beaten or flogged by their masters; the burly Indian on the pavement was *Caboclo Paraguaçú* named after a river that flows in to the bay opposite Salvador; *Sultão das Matas* (Sultan of the Jungle), an Indian man with a turban; *Iemanjá*, a voluptuous woman emerging from the sea wearing a long clingy dress. All this was to become much more familiar in time but every day as we passed the shop we wondered how this thriving establishment and the goods it sold fitted in to the smart and sophisticated modern city in which we were now living.

We grew fonder and fonder of our flat. The patio, painted a cool white, had clay pots with lush vegetation that reached to the floor above, and an old table and chairs. Inside was a motley collection of European and American antique furniture and table lamps all arranged with considerable charm and taste. There was even a silver straw for sucking mate tea out of an old gourd which the owner was kind enough to bestow upon us later as a memento with his compliments. The rattan sofa squeaked whenever we sat on it and it was some days before we discovered a family of five mice living in one of the cushions but this unpleasant inconvenience palled to insignificance beside the irrefutable fact that we had finally found a real home. We were fortunate as most of the other accommodation we saw was filled with functional plastic sofas and chairs, standard issue alas in a country that in those days would not win prizes on the world stage for interior design.

The neighbour immediately above us disapproved of

our music which drifted up to him through the potted plants despite the ludicrously low volume at which the Grundig was now permanently set. His television in the meantime boomed football commentaries at all hours and we soon learned that the numerous clubs in Rio had important matches every day. Each time a goal was scored the commentator shouted '*G-o-o-o-l*', then he gulped, filled his lungs with air, and shouted '*G-o-o-o-l*' again this time making it last for up to forty seconds. Cheers and stamping feet could be heard in all the adjoining buildings and cars and buses honked their horns. Then it was the turn of the World Cup. During the Brazil : England match we could hear our neighbour's sighs and fruity curses from our vantage point down below and he in turn could hear us good-naturedly urging on the mediocre English team and pouring scorn on Brazil's many successes. After the game we wanted to go out on to the streets to witness tickertape raining down from the upper floors in celebration of a fine victory, but when we opened our front door he was there waiting for us, a hand gun pointing at our chests, letting rip with a tirade of anti-English insults.

'Calm yourself', we said, feeling decidedly un-calm ourselves at the sight of the gun trembling with emotion in his hand. 'Brazil played wonderfully well', but this seemed to infuriate him more.

It was only when we congratulated Brazil by making it sound all the while as if he alone had been responsible for the victory, that he lowered his gun and, still shouting abuse, finally shut himself inside his flat. This had a profound effect on us. Over his shoulder was a black leather holster which made us wonder whether he was a member of the secret police. If so, we had better watch it and make sure we did nothing to annoy him in future because the secret police in Rio were renowned for their brutality. Further down our street on a main junction drivers were hooting their horns and dozens of ecstatically happy Brazilian men were urinating on the Union Jack spread out in the middle of the crossing. Hardly the sort of scene one would witness outside Lords after Australia won the Ashes.

Gay abandon of a different sort could be seen at all hours along the pavements and in the many bars and restaurants. On the one hand there was endless sophistication in dress which appealed to both of us (flares, wide leather belts with chunky buckles, silk scarves tied rakishly round the neck), and on the other an endearing habit among the *cariocas* to wander the streets in a state of considerable undress. Such unashamed indulgence in revealing the human body didn't only find its origins in the gorgeous climate but in the people themselves who were all well used to virtual nudity at carnival time and many lived within walking distance of the beach where different norms applied. Not for nothing does the great bay of Guanabara mean 'breast-shaped' in the Indian language *Guarani*. Beautiful girls in thongs and skimpy tops rode on buses and queued up at lights to cross the hectic streets while the waiting traffic snorted and snarled; older women strutted their fuller flesh along the crowded black and white mosaic pavements grasping beach balls and calling wayward grandchildren into line. Men in tightly-hugging trunks spilled out of bars and entered the marble-cool foyers where a gleaming lift would whisk them up out of the fumes. In the midst of all this city gents in suits and crisp shirts, elegant *senhoras* bedecked in gold, the young in skin-tight shirts and flowing scarves, darted and dodged along the pavements, always smart and always rewarding to perceive. Even slum dwellers near the tunnels emerged from their shacks in spotless attire and were soon lost in the general throng. Rio seemed to gather you up and sweep you along at a pace that was always jaunty, and the roaring traffic, the hiss and thump of the bus doors, and the growl of engines revving at the lights added to your sense of exhilaration and enjoyment of life. All the time, in the background, played *The Girl from Ipanema*, emerging from bars and hand-held transistors, proudly parading down the street, her footsteps mirroring the confident rhythm and poise of those who listened, followed and watched.

And yet there was great misery here too. Whole families lived in abandoned shop fronts on dark and sticky pavements surviving on charitable hand-me-downs and unwanted scraps. Others lived temporarily in new sewer pipes dumped on the beach waiting to be joined together under the sea, and there were horrific stories of children living in drains. The faces of those who looked longingly at shining goods on display were etched with lines that told of years of denial. Those with poorly paid, menial jobs who came into the city from distant slums, ill concealed their considerable burden of having to feed the many mouths they had left behind at home. In contrast to all this there were glitzy penthouses with private pools surrounded by fully-grown palm trees in over-sized glazed pots and views down the coast and over the untouched forest behind. In one of the lay-byes hidden behind some branches was a stout metal door with a complex lock and intercom giving access to a lift that went up twenty five metres then opened out in a cool and spacious sitting room with spectacular 360 degree views. Such discrepancy, unethical as it was, inevitably was pushed to the backs of our minds and after a time we, along with everybody else, came to accept it, but it tugs at our consciences even now.

Every morning I waited on the busy street in front of our building for the Bank's minibus which gave all those who lived in Copacabana a free ride into the centre. It was a little like the railway from Waterloo to Bank in that we all had our own seat and restricted our speech (always low and discreet) to the two passengers on either side. One morning the bus was in turmoil with everyone gesticulating and talking very loud. Sergio, who always sat on my left, had been visited by the death squad in the middle of the night and taken away for questioning leaving his wife and family behind. He would never return, they said, but like everyone else would become another statistic. How was it possible that such a serious and hard-working man could become involved with those who sought to overthrow the military dictatorship? Surely he knew the dangers? Sergio's father, who also worked for the Bank, sat at the back through all this in tears. After that morning the subject became taboo and was never raised again.

One bright light in the Bank was another English trainee, Piers Trumpington who had the same fears as me about being swept along a pre-conceived career path doing a job which his heart wasn't in, so we became firm buddies. I greatly admired his sense of style. No off the peg Tropiccadilly suits for him, but bespoke dark blue pinstripe in the softest and coolest cloth imaginable. In the evenings and at weekends he wore casual clothes that fitted him perfectly and made my own look tired and baggy at the knees. The shock of blonde hair that drifted down over his eyes completed the picture of a young man, ex-public school and Oxford, who knew that the world, without any undue persuasion, was his oyster. We spent our free time together, ate, drank and laughed together. Everybody loved him and in the end that turned out to be his downfall.

Into this remarkable world of glamour and privilege, aching poverty and rank ugliness stumbled, literally, down the steps of an Air France Boeing 727, my father. In his hand was the main reason for the stumble, a fishing rod. He wore a three piece tweed suit which, by the time we got him home, had to be hung up to dry. On the first day we put him in a café early in the morning with a friendly waiter and sat him down in front of a cup of coffee. I scribbled on a napkin in the International Phonetic Alphabet how to say 'Another coffee without sugar' (always a problem in Brazil where they sweeten it automatically), 'A beer please', and 'Steak and chips'. He was still there at six pm (thank Heavens) engaged in lively debate with the waiter who understood nothing but smiled and nodded as if he did, and I paid what turned out to be a very hefty bill. Clearly the waiter had understood the essentials.

We bought a mackerel and chopped off a bit every day for bait. He would then sit for hours fishing off the rocks with significant and at times embarrassing lack of success, befriending whomsoever chose to pass the time of day with him, resorting to French when really stuck as if this would make any difference. At lunchtime out would come the International Phonetic Alphabet, and in this manner he whiled away many happy hours while we went to work and very soon stopped worrying about him.

Late one afternoon we took a taxi to the monumental statue of Christ The Redeemer, winding our way up the mountain through thick jungle past enticing clusters of houses each with its unique view of the sparkling bay. Once past the souvenir vendors you emerge to a truly unforgettable 360 degree view. Behind, virgin jungle stretches to the horizon, a constant reminder of the many thousands of square kilometres of this enormous country that have still not been properly explored. To the sides and straight ahead lies Rio climbing up the steep mountains till it can climb no more, pushing out into the sea between Copacabana and the old city, sprawling north towards the international airport and even further. In front, like a Matchbox toy, is Santos Dumont airport with tiny 'planes landing and taking off purely for the enjoyment of tourists, or so it seems, banking steeply to avoid the Sugar Loaf Mountain before setting course for São Paulo and beyond. During a break in the wind a myriad of noises drifts up the mountain and over the parapet: the ring of a hammer; the barking of a dog; the toot of a car or a single shouted word. These are no more than short forays into the lives of countless thousands of people going about their business blissfully unaware that we are eavesdropping and observing, but from such a distance that they retain their dignity and their privacy. Suddenly lights are on where there were no lights before, and a quarter of an hour later the city is once again spread before us, this time a mass of shimmering colours, with distinct lines of white and red disappearing into the tunnels. It is worth the vertigo a hundredfold, the slight disappointment that the statue is too remote and too cold to be a proper Redeemer, and the grim realisation, too late, that you shouldn't have sent the taxi away. The city, so much in miniature at the top, looks curiously condensed when you join it again, and it is some time before your imagination plumps it back to its rightful size.

On Saturdays we all ate *feijoada*, a slowly-cooked casserole dish of pigs' ears, snouts and black beans served with thinly sliced orange and bright green cabbage which was a telling example of how colourful presentation can take your mind off substance. Then a lazy boat trip to Paquetá, an island at the far end of the bay where life's pace dwindles to a minimum, the internal combustion engine is not allowed and you digest your *feijoada* on a bicycle.

Just inside the entrance to our favourite restaurant on a major Copacabana thoroughfare was a pit the size of a small swimming pool filled with smouldering logs, and stuck on spits along the sides great sizzling chunks of different sorts of meat. Dining was entirely al fresco (it needed to be with that great source of heat) and round the perimeter architectural jungle plants grew loftily into the sky then threw out lianas that dangled down with fairy lanterns attached at head height. Meat arrived still sizzling on metre-long swords, strips cut off to order. Looking up from your table you could see the sides of the adjacent buildings rising like cathedrals magically lit in the overall glow.

The photograph, taken with an early Polaroid, slightly out of focus and covered with smudges, shows my father (centre) smiling broadly through the lianas during a sustaining dinner.

We frequented a late-night bar called the Crazy Rabbit written up in large polished brass letters at the door, looking clean and inviting just by the black and fumy road tunnel beneath the mountain. Inside was a small, functional bar in a corner and a grand piano surrounded by stools with room for no more than twelve. We sat round the piano each with a

long gin fizz made with crushed ice and a dollop of egg white, our glass dripping on to the lid of the piano (what would my mother think of that?), while an ebony pianist, sweat bursting from his brow, in white tuxedo, played New Orleans jazz and sang to order. My father, a great performer in his own right but more of a formal, concert pianist, sat transfixed by him, clicking his growing fingernails which for the first time ever weren't bitten to the cuticles. Late night gin with crushed ice up to the rim and a plate of cashews had become his preferred nightcap.

His new and exhilarating experiences with us seemed to energise him, and after his return to England his letters took on a refreshingly optimistic tone. I like to think Rio positively affected his spirit and left a mark because not many months after this, just weeks after our wedding in an ancient Sussex church, he was snatched away by a sudden and cruel heart attack to the utter consternation and sadness of the family and all who knew him. But way before that, during our last days in

Rio, our own lives were going to change abruptly in the same way as an earthquake can, in a minute, shift the landscape and reshape everything that is familiar.

We had suspected for some time that Piers was more attracted to men than to women, not that this affected our relationship in any way, but we were unhappy to learn that he had taken up with Rudi for the selfish reason that we would see less of him. They took a flat in Ipanema near the bar where Vinicius de Morães immortalised that girl in song and, as was inevitable, our regular evening and weekend meetings thinned to a dribble. I saw plenty of Piers at the Bank every day but he had entered another social world and was seeing a whole new group of mainly male friends. We briefly met Marcelo, a pretty young man with long black hair, olive skin and big dark eyes, and went to a party where it was obvious from the start that we were the only straight couple there. We felt uncomfortable and not terribly welcome.

When Rudi telephoned one Sunday to say that Piers was lying dead in the street we hastened to Ipanema in a taxi, speaking in whispers with numbness creeping over our brains. He was spread-eagled on his back, the brown toes of his shoes sticking up in the air, and someone had covered his head and chest. One of the neighbours in the block said she had seen a body plummet down past her window, implying that he had fallen or been pushed from the roof. Rudi, however, told us that Piers and Marcelo had recently had an affair which Piers had put a stop to and that Marcelo in a rage had shot him, driven him back to Ipanema, and pushed him unceremoniously out of the car whilst it was still moving. People down in the street were able to confirm seeing a body fly out of a fast-moving car.

When I telephoned the British Consul for advice about how to handle this crisis the first thing he asked me was whether Piers was a homosexual. He told us the Police could be brutal in their enquiries, that we would be best advised to flush down the lavatory any diary or address book that might mention us as Piers' friends, and that if he were in our shoes he would leave the country fast. He'd had plenty of experience of this sort of thing already.

We passed a sleepless night hearing odd and alarming sounds at our door (could it be the gun-happy neighbour under orders from colleagues in the Police?), sent a telegram in the morning, wrapped up our lives in Brazil in a flurry of frantic 'phone calls each of which demanded a re-telling of the previous day's ghastly events, and stepped on to a 'plane in mid afternoon, our whole world turned upside down, knowing that we were abandoning a dear friend whose time had come to such a cruel end less than twenty four hours beforehand. His picture stared at us from the *Jornal do Brasil* and the accompanying short article mentioned Rudi's name, but thankfully not ours. His death made no sense at all to us. We were still too young to acknowledge life's fragility and the shattering things that it can throw at you without warning. Still in our early twenties with the sun on our backs and our eyes on a clear horizon we fondly imagined we had tasted of immortality. The thought of Piers' mortal remains beginning to decay filled us with nothing short of horror.

9

England

The first weeks after our arrival presented difficult challenges as family and friends vied with each other for our company. News of why we had to return earlier than planned spread quickly and at each reunion we found ourselves having to tell and re-tell the haunting story of Piers' death which was a heavy burden. Nobody stopped to think that with each recollection we re-lived the horror of that afternoon in Ipanema assailed by all the attendant waves of guilt at our having abandoned him as he lay in the street. But gradually with the passage of time we learned how to filter the details that gave us most distress and on each re-telling we slowly began to find that we could control our emotions more readily. It took time before the stabbing pain of the shock diminished and we still wonder whether the consul may have been too hasty in his advice and whether we might have saved Piers' parents some of their gruesome burden if we had stayed on for a few days. A brief note arrived from Rudi saying the official Police report had been despatched to the parents in England. It was written in pencil, on torn grey paper, so hardly looked official at all, and certainly can have done nothing to help the rawness of their grief subside.

The peculiarly English reserve and obsession with politeness: how 'well' we looked, in spite of the terrible thing that had just happened, when 'brown' or 'tanned' would be so much more accurate, soon began to irritate, as indeed did 'Welcome back to civilisation' as if there was no gun crime or killing in any corner of Britain. Although one or two horrific things had happened over our two years of absence, there were aspects of life in Brazil that were lacking in England and it did not take us long to discover that we were missing them.

But we had to consider the immediate future for both of us. Where did our priorities lie now and what sort of life should we be considering? These were questions that we had been asking each other for the last two years as it became more and more clear that the Bank was not for me. We were to be married in a few weeks with all the mutual responsibilities and sense of settled permanence that that implied, and people all around were saying that marriage demanded digging a comfy hole and laying down roots. Yes, we could blow our considerable savings by buying a house (which indeed we did), acquire furniture and a car, all the trappings of those who feel they ought to settle. And yet the restless pulse of youth was still throbbing.

Was there another journey within us, more exciting and challenging than the last where we could be stretched to the limit of our emotional and material resources? This would not simply be travel but a journey of the mind involving hard mental grind, and my mind after two sterile years in the Bank needed that space very badly. We focused on having another experience from which we would hope to emerge all the wiser and more mature. But what? Nagging away in the background was the comfortable knowledge of security offered by the Bank, not to mention the prospect of a regularly increasing salary and postings throughout the luso-hispanic world. Wouldn't it be crazy to throw all that away now, and didn't I have even the slightest sense of loyalty to my employers? At that time jobs were for life and switching to another employer was comparatively rare so while convention pulled us one way, our hearts pulled us another. We had both come across at A level Pascal's renowned observation: *'Le coeur a ses raisons que la raison ne connaît point',* a rough translation of which would be that while our heart may sense the right way forward this is something which we cannot justify rationally. This pithy, finely balanced and thought provoking philosophical statement, studied by generations of students and quoted and re-quoted by thinkers and writers throughout the ages, turned out to be no more than a pretty turn of phrase when applied to our dilemma. Our hearts wanted us to take this leap into the unknown despite the voice of reason which was powerless to hold us back. Was all this just a touch self-indulgent? Weighing the different options in the balance, we seemed to get more and more confused.

The answer may not have been immediately apparent but when it arrived it came like the wind and we knew it was right for us. What I originally liked so much about the sound of the job in Honduras was, surprisingly, the lack of financial security and from the moment when the spinning coin sent me to the Bank I knew I would regret growing up too soon, becoming a faceless member of the establishment, forced to behave like everyone else. We wanted liberty and the time to read and ponder and record our thoughts. In your early twenties the attraction of security later on does not rank very high on the scale of what values are truly important in life.

So, we resolved to go back, not to Rio where things might still be tricky for us, but to Salvador where the melting pot of cultural and religious syncretism contained such a rich mixture. We would endeavour to understand the social glue binding Amerindian and African by studying their language, lore and traditions, then go on to teach with the weight of Ph.Ds behind us in the hope that, by increasing awareness, we would be doing something positive and useful. Pie in the sky? If friends and family didn't tell us directly they certainly felt it deep down. Their sage advice to keep up our National Insurance contributions fell on deaf ears, as if this were high on our list of priorities. What on earth did we think we would live on, they asked? A good question but, as Pascal had intimated, our reason was pushed to one side as our hearts took over. It's true that money worried us but I would apply for a Brazilian Government scholarship which should keep us going for a while, and Rosie would get a grant. Sager heads than ours rejected this and urged us to be more realistic but, with continuing wooliness of thought we steadfastly pursued our very unrealistic goal.

The most pressing thing to do now was for both of us to find a university to steer us in the right direction and for me to resign from the Bank.

10

Goodbye to Banking

My resignation letter prompted a swift response, a trifle too swift for my liking as I would have preferred a little more time to prepare what I wanted to say in person to the senior Staff Manager who controlled the divers careers of English staff throughout the world. Within an hour of my posting it in the Bank's Head Office internal mail I was invited to the fifth floor to discuss straight away what was troubling me as they were sure to be able to put things right. I wanted to say that I was clearly not cut out for the job, that I had often felt frustrated and let down with little, if anything, to do, that I had wasted two valuable years holding rulers whilst others drew the line, and that the two years' training could easily have been telescoped into two months.

But as soon as I entered the room I was assailed by the effusive gush of a man who, holding my file in a perfectly manicured hand, proceeded to praise my every move over the past two years (obviously he'd received no dire report from Fortaleza) and talk of instant promotion. It was as if an expensive and rare scent had been atomised into the room, a scent which I breathed in deeply then slowly exhaled, for surely this was the reserve of the gods. I was flattered and felt myself gradually becoming entrapped by the smell of sandalwood and musk. He mentioned Lisbon, Sub Manager, fat salary, and leaving within a fortnight. I was too shy in those days to ask why now, why minutes after receiving my letter, why not some months ago, but for a while played along and asked pertinent questions. I liked his answers: they lulled me as a punt filled with soft cushions lulls its occupants on a lazy summer afternoon.

I might well have weakened and accepted what he was offering but then his 'phone rang and he was out of the room for a long while. I weighed in the balance wealth, status and security on one side, and on the other, well, it all sounded like so much hot air: freedom and the attraction of adventure and discovery. It was risky and unwise to throw security out of the window and we would miss so much of what we had already accepted as the norm. Should I throw it all away now instead of pondering this latest development further? But we had already spent weeks discussing and weighing up the relative merits and de-merits of a sense of real achievement after temporary discomfort, or doing what was expected and climbing another rung. Be bold, I said to myself. Do it. There won't ever be another opportunity.

So I was bold; some might say rash. When the door opened again I said my piece politely and firmly and walked away from the Bank for ever with an unfamiliar length of stride and something akin to a swagger.

11

Douglas

Douglas was the Director of the St. Andrews University Centre for Latin American Linguistic Studies (it sounded very grand), and he was catapulted into our lives one damp and misty November evening when we sat over dinner, candle flames winking cheerily at the polished crystal, and elaborated on our plans. I say 'catapulted' because everything about him was immediate, warm and larger than life. By the end of the evening his initial interest kindled in an exchange of letters and a long 'phone call had turned into a spring tide. His gushing enthusiasm was such that he urged us to start right away: a bit of general reading first, a beginner's course in elementary *Guaraní* (the leading South American tropical forest Indian language), then a twelve month stint in and around Salvador building up a network of informants and carefully recording what they said ('One important tip: make sure your informants have teeth'), then a final year in the UK writing our theses.

Put like this, it all sounded simple and straightforward, particularly in the post-good-dinner haze with a further bottle of wine to help seal the deal. But that was his style: good food and wine set the tone. Conviviality diffused worry and concern and led to a cheerful and optimistic disposition where life's problems dwindled until they appeared very minor matters indeed.

We were charmed by all we saw and heard: a broad muscular frame, wide honest smile and a firm, bone-crushing handshake. Beneath the guffaws and hail-fellow-well-met slaps on the back was the genuineness of his love of South America and his seriousness as a scholar. Here was a man who lectured on medieval Spain while cultivating an interest in the Basque language at a time when Basque popularity was at its lowest. He was a choir master, an intimidatingly fierce squash player, a team member of Radio 4's high-brow panel game *Brain of Britain*, a colonel in the Territorial Army and an ordained priest. He was also the kindest man you could expect to meet and not surprisingly had a wide circle of friends.

'Come to coffee', he would say and every Thursday morning at eleven o'clock people flocked to his book-lined study, some grasping their own mugs, to have a cup and be party to the bubbling chat and gossip. Occasionally he would grumble at the expense of dishing out endless coffee to the ever-swelling numbers (it was always the best arabica freshly ground that morning by a posh, expensive shop in the High Street), but the grumble was just a polite reminder that you should toss a coin into the tin. The room filled with Professors and Lecturers, research students like us, undergraduates, and every now and again a distinguished visitor from the world outside like Lord Eccles, Frank Muir or John Cleese, and plenty of editors and programme makers from TV and Radio. He was always on the look out for publicity for his Centre.

The door of the cupboard where he kept the coffee machine had leather book spines pasted on the outside so that when it was shut there was no break in the books lining the walls. The titles were all serious but in the few cases where he had replaced the spines that got most wear near the knob and key-hole you could glimpse his sense of humour: *John Knox On Death's Door*, chosen for its Scottish connotations, and *Dairsie Say It Again*, a playful dig at a colleague who spent all her spare time dreaming up ways of injecting life into the damp and disused Dairsie Church some miles out in the country.

12

St. Andrews

Almost immediately we were desperately short of ready money which in turn augured very badly for our forthcoming return to Salvador in a few months' time. In fact, however, we weren't short of money at all: we were quite well off having paid for our house with a cheque and no mortgage, and we had a stash of cash in long-term deposit accounts, all remitted from Brazil during our prolonged period of plenty, but this was wealth that we didn't want to touch. We now found ourselves for the first time forced to skimp and save which, after a long period of good living, did not come easily to either of us. Our protein intake consisted of wild rabbit hunted by our dogs and squid bought from the fishmonger at knock-down prices because in those days it was sold only for cat food but somehow he learned that we didn't have a cat so pushed his price up. We prepared it with garlic, parsley and olive oil that was just beginning to appear in the shops in litre bottles and

Bringing home the protein, St. Andrews.

five litre cans. Before then it had only been available in tiny
bottles in Boots with a recommendation to use it to soften ear
wax. Vegetables were invariably large swede turnips gleaned
(or, more accurately, stolen) from the fields surrounding our
cottage.

    Rosie's grant was our one source of income and the bulk
of it went on coal, heating oil and petrol for the car which we
needed to drive in and out of St Andrews every day. I was
duly awarded a Brazilian Government scholarship which,
had it materialised, would have given us enough to survive
comfortably. Despite spending hours making expensive 'phone
calls to the Embassy in London and speaking to a wide cross
section of extremely charming and helpful people, we were told
to wait till we got to Brazil then contact the right department
there. All would be well and we needn't worry, and, yes, there

would certainly be back payments of what we had not yet received. But we never got a penny. By a cruel twist of fate I was about to experience what I had hitherto regarded as the romance of poverty, not in Honduras as Minister in Charge of Bananas, but in Brazil as a mere student.

Before leaving we sold our brand new car, making the usual huge loss, and a few other effects, and regarded the paltry sum of money we made as sufficient to last the year. Most people learn by bitter experience, and we were no exception, that figures can be massaged to support any project you may have in mind. It transpired painfully soon, while we were still in the UK, that we hadn't made anything like the right provision and we couldn't touch our long-term deposit accounts, even if we wanted to, without incurring swingeing penalties. The glittering salary that I had turned down in the Bank began to look very attractive indeed as we scratched around earning and saving what we could before our departure. Did we have a single moment of regret? Not really. Our minds were trained on the excitement of the unknown and we bravely pushed to one side any thoughts of possible future penury. We knew we had enough to survive on a very simple diet but there were all sorts of other expenses, as there always are, transport, telephone and so on, which had not entered into our reckoning. We concentrated on the long term view, the jobs with glittering prospects that would be ours for the asking. '*On n'est pas sérieux quand on a dix-sept ans...le coeur fou Robinsonne...*' Admittedly, we were a tad older than Rimbaud's seventeen year old but his suggestion that the young needn't take life seriously was still a comfort. Why shouldn't we follow our whim and wander the world like Crusoe?

It dawned on us quite soon that, in the interests of arriving in Brazil with as large a pot of money as possible to last a whole year, we would not be able to afford a standard air fare. Even steerage on a rusty cargo vessel with accommodation for a few passengers was beyond us. One of the many begging letters we wrote at the time was to Shell in London who, quite out of the blue, wrote back with an offer. None of their tankers went to Brazil, but many went to Curaçao, so would that do? My well-thumbed copy of *The South American Handbook* assured us that fares from Curaçao to Caracas in Venezuela were reasonable and we assumed that Caracas to Salvador would be within our means. The cherry on the cake was that Shell, despite our not having asked for it, undertook to transport us back to Europe when the time came. No other organisation had come up with an offer as generous as this so we decided with some alacrity to go ahead.

In order to satisfy Shell's insurers we would be employed whilst on the ship as 'supernumerary writers' at the rate of one shilling each per week. We would be given 'officer' status which meant that we would live and have our being with all the officers on the ship. No hammock then for us below decks with the men. We would probably have the cabin normally reserved for the pilot but because the ship would follow a well-known route from 'somewhere in Europe' direct to Curaçao (they couldn't yet be more specific) a pilot would not be necessary for longer than a few hours so his cabin would be free for the entire duration of the voyage. Food and accommodation would be free; alcoholic drinks for our account. The onus was on us to mention Shell's sponsorship in any future published work. Could we confirm that we were in agreement with all this? You bet we could. No dreary British Caledonian jet for us, but a gentle transfer to South America lasting a fortnight with all the on-board privileges normally given to 'officers'. We liked the idea, and we liked thinking that we were probably the only outsiders to have been offered such generous terms in the company's history.

The one downside of the whole arrangement was that they would only be able to give us one or two days' notice of the port of disembarkation so we would have to fix our affairs now and be ready to go at a moment's notice. This threw us into overdrive: 'The contents of one steamer trunk and one suitcase, and a handbag for soiled linen, meet the ordinary requirements of one person', advised the *Handbook*. But we were determined to be able to carry our own kit in case our forthcoming trip took us to far-flung areas. The thought of lugging not one, but two, steamer trunks and suitcases, not to mention two handbags, on to the roof of a bus or in to a train made up our minds. We would ignore the *Handbook*'s advice and buy a couple of knapsacks (the term 'back-pack' was not in current use at the time).

Into these, without a moment's thought about weight, we stuffed my old Grundig and a large number of cassette tapes for recording interviews with informants, a portable typewriter which despite its so-called portability weighed a ton, four index boxes filled with cards (another ton), a heavy 35m camera with lots of film and a motley assortment of clothes, stout shoes, batteries, correcting fluid, Portuguese and Yoruba dictionaries (sizeable and weighty tomes), notebooks, pens and a host of other things that we imagined might come in handy. Again our lack of experience led us to believe that having knapsacks which were too heavy didn't matter as we would never walk far with them on our backs. This was yet another serious miscalculation.

We missed the current technology age by forty years. What luxury it would have been to have a mobile with a camera, recorder and GPS combined, and a small lightweight lap-top. Even the knapsacks themselves were of sturdy heavy-duty canvas stitched to stout metal frames. There was also an elderly third bag, canvas with chunky leather trimmings, with a single shoulder strap (i.e. impossible to carry over the shoulder when carrying a knapsack) that dated from the last war and seemed to weigh some kilos even when empty. For some extraordinary reason the internal set of luggage wheels that today glide so effortlessly along pavements, hadn't yet been invented. Meanwhile, top-heavy and hopelessly over-encumbered like bag people on city streets, we assumed we had thought of everything, until the *Handbook* again gave us further reason for concern. On board ship in the tropics '... light tennis clothing with cellular or thin woollen underwear is recommended. Cotton frocks in colours which withstand strong light and sea air are most serviceable, and rubber-soled shoes should be included.' We definitely had no room for any of that. The paragraph about excursions in the Amazon forest wearing 'thin khaki breeches and shirt...leggings and ankle boots' made us think we should perhaps have opted for the steamer trunks after all in order to accommodate extra vital equipment among which were 'Rubber-flanged tin boxes containing some 56lb employed for packing any spare effects'. We had every intention of spending a good deal of time in remote parts and were concerned that we were leaving very ill-prepared with no rubber flanges whatsoever.

And so we awaited our summons. May and June came and went. Every time we washed clothes we worried they wouldn't dry in the unpredictable Scottish summer weather before our summons arrived. We rang and checked they had our 'phone number. July. Then suddenly, as if an army officer in the trenches had blown a whistle, a telegram: 'Dublin, berth X, 11:00 hours Wednesday'. There was no time to take stock. We had thirty six hours before our ship sailed and in spite of all the waiting still had to organise our journey to Ireland, deliver our dogs to a friend on standby, cope with a pile of damp washing (yes, the inevitable had happened) and tie up a host of other unforeseen loose ends before shutting the cottage door behind us and manhandling our ill-conceived luggage into a crowded commuter train to Edinburgh.

13

Partula

Within hours we were in the air again savouring the gently lilting Irish accent of the air hostess, hardly believing that we had finally left on the first stage of our journey. The excitement of the unknown is all very well but it bears with it a good deal of fear too. We knew Brazil intimately but had moved only in privileged circles and had never dealt directly with the poor. Why should they welcome us and why indeed should they devote time and effort imparting their knowledge and experience to us when we were the only ones who stood to benefit? Was this whole venture a big mistake? The latest news from another research student on the Bolivian *Altiplano* was that, while transcribing a tape-recording in Quechua of villagers' chat, he had heard in the background a plot to assassinate him that night. How sure could we be that such a horror was not going to happen to us? Perhaps the most alarming thing of all which ached dully in the pit of our stomachs was the thought that we had grossly under-estimated the difficulty of gathering together enough original material to complete our Ph.Ds. Douglas' last words to us were that we were about to make our very own 'contribution to knowledge'. We both found that scary as it meant that we had to discover something new and write a great deal about it. We couldn't keep asking Douglas' advice as we already knew how slow and unreliable the postal service to and from Brazil was. We were on our own and very much in charge of our destiny.

Shell arranged for us to sleep in a seamen's hostel which was close enough to the docks to ensure we reached the ship in good time the following morning. It was a run-down establishment with no foyer, just a slab of wood inside the door behind which sat the proprietor gazing forlornly at a small ill-tuned television. Our room was drab, smelt musty and damp, with a greasy bathroom down the corridor, but compared to some of the places we were about to discover it was a veritable palace. Everything was brown, including the wallpaper, and the carpet had holes through to the floorboards. From the window came the mournful blast of ships' horns providing a constant reminder of why we were here and not in our dry, comfortable cottage with its wide views over the countryside and the distant sea. We remembered it all with a stab of nostalgia and spoke of what we might have seen and learned by the time we returned in the space of a year. But we were talking in a vacuum and had no clear idea of what lay in store.

All this may have been very invigorating but we were also full of nervous anticipation that was not helped by the disturbing sight of bullet holes in Dublin's stone façades and the leaden sky. We gulped down cellar-cold draught Guinness in a long narrow pub full of men with grey faces, looking long and hard at us and talking in low tones. Killing time in a new country is never as thrilling as it might be. You dare not stroll too far from where you are staying in case you forget the way back and you feel you have to keep half an eye on strangers muttering in dark corners who might be about to pounce and steal your money and passport. Predictably we ate in a lowly dive close to our hostel which smelled of chip fat with a small selection of lonely, silent diners. Dublin for us was no more than a departure lounge where we eagerly waited for the next stage of our journey to begin. We had never been on an ocean-going ship before, just a cross-Channel ferry, nor had we ever had a cabin. Every fibre of our beings was taut in expectation of the moment when our tanker would untie and set off towards another world.

The following morning we managed somehow, by carrying the third bag between us, each with a hand on the one shoulder strap, to walk the short distance to the docks, followed by a worryingly long distance past berth after berth looking anxiously for ours, cursing the crippling weights on our backs which considerably impeded progress. We made it just in time. A sailor, observing our clumsy progress up the very narrow gangplank with a critical eye, led us to a metal gangway that went from one end of the ship to the other, preceded us along it, took us down a virtually vertical stair and flung open a door. We hardly had time to off-load and take a cursory glance at our new home when the door opposite ours opened and there was the Captain with a smart salute saying 'Welcome aboard'. He invited us in, told us of the importance of punctuality at meal times, showed us with some pride the switch-on-the-logs electric fire in a 1950's wooden fireplace surround, and asked why he had the honour of transporting us to Curaçao. We stumbled over our words and found it very difficult to justify how our proposed research had any worth, but his questions kept coming. By the time we left him we were convinced we would be the talking point of the Officers' mess over lunch and dinner. They would no doubt consider us an odd addition to the ship's company. As we unpacked, the gnawing doubt returned but the throb of the engines, the noise of urgent feet outside our door and a hint of movement through the window soon had us out in the open air watching as men untied ropes, wound in chains, and set us free from the dockside. In a surprisingly short while the grey Atlantic took us into its swell and we rolled around unsteadily with no sensible rhythm and a definite feeling that we had lost the use of our legs.

We had free run of the ship though we were told that we would not be welcome in those areas reserved for 'the men'. The only way you could walk the length of the ship and move between our cabin and the mess was along the metal gangway with, mercifully, high railings along the sides. Beneath you were the tanks with their inspection hatches and filler pipes with shiny brass caps. At the bow was a small plunge pool about two metres square which, most irritatingly, remained empty for the duration of the voyage. Wherever you went outside there was an overwhelming smell of bitumen and it was only at the sharpest point of the bow that you could breathe uncontaminated air.

Our well-appointed cabin was second only to the Captain's in size and quality of furnishings. We had a desk where we could do our 'supernumerary writing', comfortable armchairs fixed to the floor with a chain, and an *en suite* bathroom, not forgetting magnificent views over the bow and to starboard. Outside our door was a small area out of the wind just large enough for a couple of chairs. Here we sat after dinner on our first night nursing a whisky, gazing at the lights of Ireland winking in the distance and hoping that we would soon get accustomed to the lurching movement of the ship. We had learned from officers and their wives over dinner that each Shell tanker bears the name of a shell and ours was a bitumen carrier called Partula, which is a small brown and cream snail about half an inch long, also known as the Tahitian tree snail. Just outside the Mess was a smart glass and wooden cabinet fixed to the wall at eye height with an enlarged model of the snail displayed inside. Our Partula, like the snail, was small (19,500 tons), and this, together with the fact that the tanks were empty, probably accounted for the ship's unruly passage through the sea.

The dining room, known as the dining saloon, had good quality 1950s furnishings, wood panelling on the walls and a carpet with bold diagonal stripes. There were two unwritten rules: choose fast; eat even faster. This was not the place to linger over the menu card weighing the pros and cons of Dover Sole and Lancashire hot pot. You were expected to speed read and blurt out your order. The usual restaurant conventions were ignored. At the same table a fast-eater would move onto his pudding while the rest were still in the middle of their main course. We discovered that in order to save everybody's valuable time at breakfast we should behave just like them, ignoring the menu card and saying curtly to the waiter 'Breakfast'. This resulted in one of everything being brought to the table so you could pick and choose and, provided you remembered to eat fast, no-one batted an eyelid. At the end of lunch and dinner which were formal meals (the men wore jackets and ties; I was granted dispensation because, in defiance of the *Handbook*, I had only brought tee shirts and a pullover), the Captain would place both hands palm down on the table, look round at his fellow diners and say 'Shall we'? This was the signal for all to rise. The younger and more sprightly repaired to the smoking room next door which was presided over by a very large picture of the Queen.

Every two or three days a sheet, torn in one corner, was draped over a wire in a corner of the smoking room, and a projector placed precariously on a chair in the corner opposite. We and the officers would arrive first and sit in the more comfortable armchairs then 'the men' would file in and settle down on hard stacking chairs to watch the film. One of them swore when he tripped over the projector wire plunging the room into darkness. He was immediately reprimanded by an officer and the room fell quiet again. The discipline might have been exemplary but most of the films left much to be desired: slapstick comedy, drawn-out romances with lengthy kissing scenes and a haunting murder story set in France where the investigating *gendarme* whom everyone trusted turned out to be the killer of the two beautiful girls on a cycling holiday.

The Chief Engineer, whom I only ever saw smartly attired in full uniform in the Mess, invited me down to the engine room. The heat and noise were dreadful and the men, including the Chief Engineer himself, were all stripped to the waist and working very hard. I had suspected that once the engines were up and running there wouldn't be very much left for people to do but here, four or five half-naked grimy men were shinning up ladders, tweaking levers and shouting out the readings on a myriad of dials and instruments. While I watched, orders came from the bridge to change course two or three times. No wonder these people had such an appetite, and to don a uniform after a few hours working in such conditions must have been distinctly pleasurable. I was already feeling out of place wearing just a tee shirt for formal meals; Rosie too wished there had been room in our luggage for one or two formal outfits. But we already knew that even in the social circles where we used to move, Brazil's dress code was always very informal. I remembered with a pang that I had worn my tuxedo only once in two years for a pompous dinner that we gave in our flat. That was the occasion when the maid laughed out loud when she saw it and said I looked like a waiter.

We befriended 'Sparks', the radio operator who worked in a small windowless room and received messages in Morse Code on strips of paper that spewed out of a slit in the front of the radio. He also had a radar screen and could identify each green pin-prick as we approached. The short wave radio picked up news broadcasts from England so he was able to keep abreast of County cricket scores and general news headlines which he pinned up on a board. He held very traditional and conservative views about a number of things and was for ever quoting Nancy Mitford's *Noblesse Oblige*, especially the essay *U and Non-U* (U for upper class) which pin-pointed salient aspects of English social behaviour and speech in 1950s Britain. He went even further and established the 'Pen-Clubber class', those that did and those that did not hold their knife as if it were a pen. He chuckled uncontrollably as he divided the mess up along these lines. All this was harmless enough and he was at heart an amiable man who took a shine to us probably because we were about the same age as his own children whose company he missed.

One day the Captain summoned us to the bridge and asked a favour. Would it be possible for us to interpret for a seaman, a native of the Azores, who couldn't make himself understood to the officer who supervised the men's pay. We agreed to this with alacrity as there were precious few opportunities for us to show our appreciation of everyone's kindness. The man was brought to the bridge where he came into the company of a number of gold-braided officers whose presence made him so awestruck that during the first minutes of the conversation we had to urge him to speak up clearly as we couldn't hear or understand what he was saying. His Portuguese was more akin to that of the Mother Country, full of swallowed vowels and consonants to which our ear was not well accustomed and as he spoke he turned his head to stare in awe at the gold braid, so comprehension was a major problem. After some time we were able to ascertain that he wished to remit part of his pay back to his family in the Azores but couldn't because his papers weren't entirely in order. The overseeing officer could see no way around this so the hapless Azorean was led away below decks and we were left feeling that somehow we had let both sides down.

After two days we were used to the ship's ungainly rolling and went for thrilling walks up and down the central metal gangway trying to get some exercise in the bitumen-laden air. We would grab the railings and watch the Atlantic rollers breaking over the sides and meeting beneath us in a foamy slap and crash that sent columns of grey and white water above our heads. There seemed to be no way of attaching ourselves to the metal railings. Indeed, members of the crew trotted along the gangway with no fear, dodging the foam as best they could, and yet a rogue wave would have had no difficulty bearing us all up and over the railing into the boiling waters on the other side. We always left the cabin together so that one of us could raise the alarm if anything untoward were to happen. No doubt nowadays our being accepted as passengers on a tanker with no adequate safety provision would be condemned by Health and Safety who for once, in this instance, might have had a point. But there was a great thrill to be had feeling the ship pitching, tossing and rolling with us very much out there, wind, spray and foam in our faces, soaked to the knees, holding on to each other and shouting to make ourselves heard above the din. Between us and the horizon nothing but great waves passing sluggishly by like living mountains moving in slow motion, each full of a fearsome energy to be unleashed on some foreign shore.

Once we were well away from the continent the wild movement of the ship diminished just a little and the sea for the first time since our departure lost its dull greyness and began to look blue. We saw dolphins rolling gracefully along beside us and on the day that the crew changed out of their blue uniforms into white summer kit we saw from our vantage point just outside our cabin door a shoal of flying fish moving in the same direction and at the same speed as us, brown in colour but glinting brightly whenever the sun caught them. One night as we sat looking out to sea our view was of patches of phosphorescence, an eerie green glowing as if lit by shoals of mermaids bearing torches far beneath it.

All these new experiences, delightful though they were, were not sufficient to make the long days pass more quickly. The voyage from Dublin to Curaçao took only twelve days but we found shortly after leaving that there were long stretches of every day with precious little to do, and the rolling of the ship was not conducive to reading for more than a few minutes at a time. The officers' wives felt the same and we would gather for coffee, tea or pre-dinner drinks in order to while away the time. The wives felt particularly hard done by, though they all agreed that being on the ship with their husbands was much preferable to whiling away the empty weeks of separation at home. It was cheaper too because when on board they had no living expenses so every penny of the husband's salary could be saved. There were small indications in their cabins of the female touch: framed family photographs; a curtain on a makeshift pole over the port hole; potted plants and home-made cake which the chef allowed them to make in his galley kitchen at quiet times between shifts. We were quite a community: a group of housewives (with two stray 'supernumerary writers') living in the marine equivalent of a cul de sac, gossiping, preening, comparing and waiting for the moment when they would be allowed out to the big Shell store in the Curaçao docks where they would stock up on English delicacies to feed to their men folk. One regular complaint was that there was too much to eat, nowhere to exercise (we never came across them on our so-called walks, and the exercise bike bolted to the deck next to the pool remained unused) and everyone put on too much weight.

The Partula was so unlike any ship we had sailed on before that when the first dark green smudge of Curaçao appeared on the horizon we half expected the falsetto voice of a young lad in the Crow's Nest to shout out 'Land Ahoy'. In fact, no-one shouted anything but there was a stirring from all quarters as the crew made their preparations. Crates and boxes appeared from inner recesses and were stacked on either side of the break in the rail where the gangway would eventually be placed. The wives washed each other's hair and applied more make-up than usual although each knew that they would only have four hours' shopping on shore. We were advised to pack and be ready to disembark when told to do so. We docked at eleven in the morning and as soon as the ropes and chains were in place local dockers jumped on to the ship, undid the brass caps to the bitumen tanks, attached greasy black filler pipes and started pumping. A blue hose was attached further along the side for water. Seamen stood at the top and foot of the gangway like policemen directing traffic up and down: crates of fresh vegetables and cardboard boxes of other supplies, beer and rum. The wives were let off in a gaggle, clouds of perfume overcoming briefly the all-pervading smell of bitumen. They cut a fine dash against the dusty black of the dockside and made their way directly to the Shell shop, a corrugated iron building where they were to do the first leg of their shopping.

And then it was our turn, struggling down with our ungainly loads, looking out for a representative from Shell who would be waiting by the gate. It was a long time before we got there, forced to walk at a snail's pace because of the crippling weight on our shoulders and the heavy, humid tropical air, but there was indeed a man there and he had some excellent news.

Shell were to put us up at a hotel for the night then take us to the airport the next afternoon for our flight to Salvador. He handed us an envelope in which were our tickets. Shell were going to pick up the bill for everything.

The taxi sped away from the port towards Willemstad, capital of the Netherlands Antilles and of the island of Curação. On the back shelf blared a loudspeaker in *Papiamento*, a mixture of Spanish, Portuguese and Dutch so we were able more or less to follow what was being said. When we spoke slowly to the driver in Spanish and Portuguese he half understood what we were saying and gave us a running commentary of what was going on outside the windows. Houses in the suburbs were of gaily-painted corrugated iron with flowers at the windows and a good deal of dust and hubbub along the street. Nearer the centre, the Dutch influence was marked with fine seventeenth century gabled houses and in the main shopping centre, called Punda, the streets narrowed to just five metres wide and were lined with fine shops shortly to be patronised no doubt by Partula wives.

Our hotel was just out of the centre of town along a quiet shady street with a view past Reception to a glittering white sandy beach where there were tables and coconut matting sunshades fluttering in the breeze. We felt very grand ordering drinks and lunch, toes buried in the sand, knowing full well that somebody else would be picking up the bill. The hotel was of the superior kind and our room had its own *en suite* bathroom. The *Handbook*, on the other hand, had prepared us for '...bathrooms...some distance from the sleeping quarters...Moreover, there is in many cases no accommodation for dressing in the bathrooms themselves'. As the hotel was virtually empty I was tempted to ask them to change our room which looked over the street to one that had sea views, but we didn't take long to decide not to look this particular gift horse in the mouth. You can imagine our dismay when, checking out the following day after a superb dinner and another lunch, the receptionist handed us the bill and demanded payment, but a quick 'phone call magically settled matters and we were soon on our way to the airport.

14

Brazil again

It was a strange feeling indeed to be on the last leg of our journey back to Brazil when we had left it in such terrible circumstances only a few months previously, but Salvador was well over a thousand kilometres from Rio and we knew that the ghosts of that experience couldn't follow us there. Out of the windows on both sides was the thick mat of jungle stretching relentlessly for mile upon mile. Then the great mouth of the Amazon, the brown stain reaching far out into the Atlantic, followed again by thick jungle much of which has since disappeared, with the occasional tantalising clearing in which probably were the huts, invisible to the naked eye from this height, of a tribe who were totally unaware of what lay beyond their territory. We, on the other hand, expected that over the coming months we would be meeting plenty of people jealously guarding the secrets of their ancestors with links to African tribes, Yoruba speaking in the majority, tribes that only stopped being a source of slaves for the Brazilian market in 1888.

Eighty three years ago. No time at all actually. In fact, there were almost certainly ex-slaves still alive who could remember the moment of liberation. They would have been born slaves in Brazil so only their ancestors long since dead would have remembered the horror of the slave ships where up to twenty per cent died of diseases and maltreatment during the course of the voyage. There were equal horrors awaiting them in the sugar plantations: not just a lifetime of crippling hard labour but physical abuse from their masters who whipped them into action and shackled them to keep them at bay. Etchings of these instruments of torture are a grim reminder that the white masters at the time regarded their slaves as members of a sub-species with no feelings or emotions of their own. Animals attached to the big house, dogs, poultry, cows, were treated with considerable respect, and yet without slaves the virgin jungle could not have been cleared, nor could the ever-bountiful harvests have been collected.

In time such grievous violence towards the slaves gradually diminished but the level of injustices, although not based on physical violence, continued to reinforce the white man's superiority over his workforce. Very often the white master and his sons deliberately infected their slave women with syphilis, that peculiarly white man's disease, in the mistaken belief of the time that there was no better purge for it than a young black virgin. According to a Dr. Macedo writing in 1869, this 'barbarous superstition' held that 'the inoculation of a pubescent female with this virus is the surest means of extinguishing it in oneself'.

Since Abolition Afro-Brazilians have recovered a good deal of their self-esteem and while it might be an exaggeration to say that Caucasians and other races live in perfect harmony, it is certainly true that there is significantly less racial tension in Brazil than elsewhere. There are a number of reasons why this should be the case. Syphilis or no, many slaves' masters took liberties with their slave women and the resulting *mulatto* children were often integrated in both the white and black communities of the household. Unlike in North America, many white infant children were left with black wet nurses and unbreakable bonds were thus established not only between nurse and child but between the white child and the children of slaves in the household. The Portuguese Court and Catholic Church showed tolerance merely by insisting that all slaves should be baptised and receive instruction in basic Christian beliefs, including a brief history of the lives of the saints. Nothing more was required of them apart from a short morning service on some plantations before the day's work began. Mild tolerance was also shown towards the traditional beliefs and practices which the Africans brought with them. In fact, the development of the cults was openly encouraged in order to maintain a high level of contentment among the work force provided that the faithful, on the surface at least, switched allegiance from the pagan deities to their Catholic counterparts. In this way, the Catholics could save face, and the Africans, late at night in their own quarters, were free to worship their deities and keep their beliefs alive. There was no great stake driven between the two religions. On the contrary. Each grew to recognise and respect the similarities in the other.

Early Portuguese and Italian settlers, fleeing poverty

at home, were simple fishermen or untutored artisans who were just as deeply imbued as the Africans with age-old pagan beliefs. Such superstitions and beliefs had already become incorporated into their Christian year and practice and were such an integral part of their lives that the Church, despite the grip of the Inquisition and widespread witch trials, could do little to stamp them out. These people who went over to Brazil in large numbers from the early days right the way through to Abolition in 1888 and beyond found integration with the Africans and acceptance of their religious beliefs seamless and straightforward. The result was an immediate tolerance and acceptance of African culture and belief which persists to the present day. Unlike the United States that also imported countless thousands of African slaves, Brazil has never had a race riot and, although there certainly is a divide dictated by wealth where the majority of the poor continue to be the black descendants of slaves or *mulattos*, Brazilian society is a model of harmony and mutual respect. When the Brazilian poor riot and loot supermarkets it is primarily because they are hungry.

15

Some gods

The veneration of the crucified Jesus at the moment of his death is an old Portuguese tradition taken to Brazil in 1740 when a Portuguese captain carried a statue of the dead Jesus from Setúbal (home of the famous and long-lived sweet white wine) to Salvador. The arrival of the statue, (not the wine), inspired the foundation of a religious order and the subsequent building of Salvador's most famous church *Nosso Senhor do Bonfim* (Our Lord of the Good End) in 1754. Although on the surface this is a Catholic church like any other it has over time become the most powerful symbol of syncretism between the Christian and the African traditions. Jesus, being the incarnate form of the Son of Almighty God, was perceived by the Africans as the closest equivalent to *Oxalá*, one of the most important of all Yoruba gods and the son of the Yoruba supreme being *Olodumaré*. Like Jesus he dresses in white, has a calm and soothing character, and commands an enormous following.

On the Feast of *Bonfim* (January 6) crowds of women gather outside the church and perform a traditional Yoruba cleansing dressed in *Oxalá*'s costume, dancing and singing his chants. The church is a major centre of healing and has a chapel packed full of *ex votos* (small paintings, and plaster casts of body parts) left as offerings by the faithful. This derives from an ancient European practice whereby the faithful make a vow to offer to the church a specially commissioned picture or a plaster representation of the afflicted part of the body that has now been healed, hence the term *ex voto* which means 'resulting from a vow'. But here the 'faithful' are not necessarily only devout Catholics to the exclusion of other influences: they see in the person of Jesus an acceptable replica of *Oxalá* which is why they wear white, sing his traditional Yoruba chants and ritualistically wash the church's steps.

Ex voto offerings, Bomfim church, Salvador.

The Catholic priests of *Bomfim* Church tolerate this extraordinary situation and view it as no more than a harmless, misguided and ignorant extension of the belief that Jesus has the power to heal the sick, but the faithful believe wholeheartedly that Jesus and *Oxalá* are one and the same person. *Oxalá* is given just as much credit as Jesus for a successful healing.

If you compare Butler's very sober *Lives of the Saints* with the colourful swashbuckling biographies of the Yoruba gods that have come down to us via oral tradition you can see why and how the links between them were originally made. There is always a similarity, however tenuous, between the familiar Christian saint and the Yoruba god which at one level at least shows that people from diametrically different cultures always ask the same questions about their existence and look to divine beings to ease the burden of their daily lives.

The Virgin Mary, whose miraculous conception is one of the Mysteries of the Church, has, since early times, been called *Stella Maris*, Star of the Sea, a star to be followed on life's journey towards final union with Christ. St. Bernard of Clairvaux (12th century) wrote: "If the winds of temptation arise, if you are driven upon the rocks of tribulation, look to the star, call on Mary. If you are tossed upon the waves of pride, of ambition, of envy, of rivalry, look to the star, call on Mary. Should anger, or avarice, or fleshly desire violently assail the frail vessel of your soul, look at the star, call upon Mary." *Yemanjá* and *Oxun*, goddesses who guarantee fertility and protect seafarers, constitute at first sight an obvious link with the Virgin Mary who, in defiance of the laws of nature, conceived miraculously, but that is where the likeness ends. These two goddesses have many other attributes that could never be associated with Mary. They flick a fan seductively, are idle and vain and attract attention from their admirers by shaking their many shiny metal necklaces and bracelets in order to make a din. They are soaked in perfume, their lips smothered in lipstick which they constantly check with a mirror that never leaves their hand. These foibles bring them closer to us because we can see ourselves in many of them. Here are two deities with so many human characteristics we find endearing and almost amusing that we can virtually reach out and touch them. Other *orishás*, with their dominion over thunderbolts and lightning, war, disease and fire, we have to treat with a healthy dose of respect and, above all, keep our distance.

The woman I had seen in the market when I was first in Salvador as a Bank trainee went into trance on seeing a picture of Saint Barbara. The more I learned about the syncretism between African gods and Christian saints the easier it was to understand what precisely had happened. The picture of Saint Barbara triggered a memory within her of her initiation into the cult and this alone was sufficient to send her into a trance. Initiation procedures are long and complex, and involve the initiate staying in the cult house learning everything there is to know about their god, or *orishá* as the gods are called in Yoruba: the drum rhythms, the chants, the food and herbs. These details become so ingrained in the mind and memory of the initiate that when they leave the cult house to live in the outside world after initiation a picture, sound or smell can act as the trigger that makes them fall into a trance. Just hearing the drum rhythm, smelling one or two of the herbs, or indeed glancing at a picture is sufficient. The belief is that the god to whom you 'belong' uses you as a medium and can then be consulted about how best to cure an illness or resolve a dilemma, so when somebody falls into a trance they forsake their normal worldly identity and, for a spell, become a god with considerable power to improve our lot on earth.

It is no wonder that the African slaves saw an immediate link between their own *Yansan* and Saint Barbara. *Yansan* is hyperactive and the goddess of wind, storm, hurricane and tempest and can deliver a lightning bolt with a wave of her hand. The colour with which she is most closely linked is red (all devotees wear red costumes), and red is naturally associated with the high temperatures and fever which she is invoked to cure. It follows that in Brazil she is the patron of firemen who have pictures of *Yansan* or Saint Barbara on display inside their fire engines which are of course red. She gets what she wants and any difficulties are immediately surpassed. Her dance movements involve the arms brushing away evil forces with considerable ease.

As women go, both *Yansan* and Barbara are forceful characters and not to be trifled with. Take Barbara's name for example. It is an unfortunate name for a future saint to be saddled with because it means 'barbarian, savage, uncivilised and coarse', none of which would be an appropriate description of Barbara. Her unpleasant father, however, was all those things so we must assume that his earliest wish was to visit upon his daughter all the unfortunate characteristics which he saw in himself. It's a great shame that Barbara's mother, who might have had some sway over him, doesn't figure at all in the legends.

Father was rich and pagan (a fitting combination for a

man of his dire attributes in a Christian legend) and he was very wicked for he kept his daughter locked up in an impregnable stone tower and never let her out. His main concern was that she might come into contact with good people and possibly drift away from him. He wasn't at all worried when he went on his long journey because the tower was solid and the door of iron. Barbara prayed and prayed and when her father eventually returned she declared that she was now a Christian and would happily die for her beliefs. Father in a mighty rage drew his sword in order to put an end to his treacherous daughter but, and here the legend is quite clear, the wall of the tower miraculously parted (without the tower collapsing) and Barbara was able to slip away leaving her father shouting that he would catch up with her and chop off her head. Barbara's bright red dress made it impossible for her to hide and the State governor soon caught up with her and started to have her tortured in the most ghastly way, leaving her dripping with blood every evening. His plans were thwarted however because every morning after the torture of the previous day all her cuts and wounds had miraculously healed. Father, always an impatient and impetuous man, cut off her head with just one blow of his sword, but on his way home was struck by a thunderbolt and died instantly. With a bit more foresight he might have seen that coming.

Nobody remembers him today but his daughter became quite a celebrity. Powder magazines on ships were called *Santa Bárbaras* because sailors kept a small statue of her standing next to her tower inside the magazine to protect the ship from exploding. She became the patron of armourers, military engineers, gunsmiths, miners, stonecutters and anyone whose work might expose them to a violent or sudden death. On her feast day (December 4th) she is honoured by the UK Royal Artillery and the RAF Armourers. On the same day the Greek army and Cypriot National Guard offer visitors *loukoumades*, a traditional sweet that resembles cannonballs. The medallion of the US Order of Saint Barbara (US Field Artillery Association) shows the saint and her tower on one side, and a cannon with a pile of cannonballs on the other. In many respects Barbara and *Yansan* are a perfect match.

It is often said by those with experience in such matters that two people with very similar characters, shouldn't get married. *Xango* and *Yansan*'s marriage must have been at best stormy, at worst a veritable clash of the Titans. They both control lightning, thunderbolts and fire and have tempestuous

Yansan.

personalities. We can well imagine the unholy clashes unleashed when they are both at it hammer and tongs. Add to this the undeniable fact that *Xango* also controls war and you have a marriage that may indeed have been made in Hell. But we like our gods to be fierce, to get their way, and never to yield.

Xango is regarded as old and mature, quick-tempered perhaps, but with sufficient wisdom to ensure his behaviour never results in chaos. He is linked to St. Jerome because the two are regarded by their followers as old and wise thinkers whose decisions are based on wide experience of the world, and in Jerome's case at least, extensive and thorough reading. Where Jerome constantly wields his pen extolling, among other things, the value of celibacy and virginity, *Xango* carries a double-headed axe with which he delivers swift and balanced justice. The link is not as obvious as with other African gods and Catholic saints (Jerome for example is far from stormy, and although he never says as much, he abhors war), but they do share seniority and command considerable respect.

Omolú wears a face mask, sometimes an entire robe made of straw, to hide his dreadful and pestilential sores, and he walks stooped like a sick man in pain, with slow, uneven gestures. He is the Yoruba equivalent of Lazarus who lay suffering from illness outside the rich man's house but, poor fellow, was not even given crumbs from the rich man's table. The story has a happy ending, however, when Lazarus finally dies from his ailments and, lulled in Abraham's bosom, looks down on the rich man burning in Hell. *Omolú* is also linked with St. Roche who is often depicted lifting his robe to reveal suppurating plague wounds (an all too common affliction in medieval times) licked clean by an obliging dog. Born rich, he

Omolú hiding his sores.

waited till his parents died then distributed all his wealth among the poor (arguably the main reason for *Omolú's* popularity among the lower echelons of Brazilian society), and became a mendicant pilgrim on the road to Rome. He ministered to all those suffering from the plague and eventually, as you would expect, got it himself.

He is now the patron saint of dogs (who, more than anyone, need a patron saint when the canine chips are down), diseased cattle, falsely accused people, invalids, and the very unlikely foursome of surgeons, bachelors, gravediggers and second-hand dealers. Would second-hand car dealers be included I wonder?

You might not think that St. George, that veritable bastion of Englishness, would have his equivalent in the Yoruba pantheon, but he does. *Oxossi* is the god of the hunt and wears green, the colour of the jungle. It is a relatively short leap from killing a dragon to hunting the daily meat and whereas St. George is always depicted with a sword or lance piercing his prey, *Oxossi* carries the huntsman's main tools, a bow and arrow. Adherents to his cult tend to be sharp like the arrow, astute and intelligent. The plant most closely associated with him is the green and yellow agave (*sansevieria trifasciata laurentii*) with a vicious pin-prick point at the end of the leaf and smaller spikes all along the edges. The leaves are thought to bear a remarkable resemblance to St. George's spear, and if you trip up over the plant (a most unpleasant experience which I often had because it is grown in pots outside front doors) you can spend hours with tweezers extracting the spines.

Ogun (St. Anthony) has a similar plant (*sansevieria zeylanica*) with the same shaped leaves but these are blue-grey and since they are similarly endowed with punishing needles should only be approached with gloves on. *Ogun* is the god of iron and of blacksmiths, and he carries a sword (in the vernacular his plant is called the Sword of *Ogun*). He is linked to St. Anthony because he can, by swinging his sword from side to side, open up paths and remove difficulties as Anthony is believed to help locate things that have got lost.

In all these cameos of the Yoruba pantheon of deities and Christian saints there is always at least one thing, however

Greeting Ogun.

insignificant or small, that establishes the link. The Africans in their slave quarters, wanting in their misery to invoke their own gods from Africa, latched on to whatever first presented itself in the life of a Christian saint that could serve as the link they needed. Once the slaves were able to refer to their god by the equivalent saint's name the Church was sufficiently satisfied and, by extension, so were the slaves' masters. The day started with invocations and prayers in the chapel led by the estate chaplain or the master himself; it ended behind the locked doors of the slave quarters when drumbeats, chants and the smells and scents of herbs called upon the gods to come down and incorporate themselves in the bodies of the faithful. The slave quarters were the first cult houses; the slaves that were most highly skilled in the traditional practices became the first priests and priestesses. After Abolition cult houses sprang up all over the City and the priests and priestesses, now known as Fathers or Mothers of the Saints, took on the onerous task of initiating the young, healing the sick and protecting their flock from the ever-present forces of evil.

Our main task in Salvador and small towns all around was to contact these houses, befriend the hierarchy and their followers, and observe them all at work. Some immediately allowed us in with our tape recorder and camera; others were more reticent and guarded their secrets, feeling, quite understandably, that a secret divulged might result in less efficacious cures. We gradually gained their confidence. Speaking the language and involving ourselves in their everyday concerns helped enormously so eventually we were invited to as many cult houses as we wished to observe, ask questions and note down our findings. The cult of the dead on Itaparica island, however, remained closed to us until our last few days on the island when we were invited (at dead of night so we would not remember the path by day) to climb up to the cult house hidden from sight at the top of a steep hill among the towering trees and thick vegetation.

We were frequently the first outsiders to witness the extraordinary things that took place in all these cult houses and what we learned was so new at the time and so unusual that we often had to stop in our tracks and wonder where it would all end. Friends and family seriously worried whether we were becoming besotted by it all. Had we discovered a religion that was offering more than the religious tradition in which we had been raised in the UK? Might we go the whole hog and request initiation into one of the cult houses? No, we would not, we could not do that, but this did not quell their anxieties. Even if we had wanted to have the experience of going into trance we learned very early on that our religious upbringing and childhood conditioning erected a psychological barrier which made it impossible. So we never did.

The two or three biggest and richest cult houses in Salvador featured on glossy tourist maps and were accustomed to coach-loads disgorging their over-excited (usually American) passengers after a good dinner at their hotel, then meeting them a couple of hours later gleefully holding their reels of spent film. There was no point at all in our visiting such places: their work had been well documented; they had distinguished patrons among whom were Jorge Amado, the renowned novelist whose plots are mainly set in and around Salvador, University professors and even the State Governor. Some of the priestly hierarchy appeared occasionally on television. Dona Olga de Alaketu, Mother of the Saints and leader of one of these houses, was appointed by the government in Brasília to visit Nigeria as a sort of cultural ambassadress. She was all over the newspapers when she left and, when she returned, the visit was hailed as a great success. One fascinating detail skipped over in the press was that when she first opened her mouth to speak Yoruba, a language she had learned in the cult house handed down by countless preceding generations, the modern Nigerians found it quaint, as we might find Elizabethan English quaint were we to have the opportunity of meeting a real Elizabethan. Our business, however, was with smaller and poorer cult houses so we could observe how the lower strata of Brazilian society in the suburbs, villages and small towns used the cult house as a place of healing. Some of the stories in the press about miraculous cures were tantalising and we hoped to be able to see these things for ourselves.

16

Dona Cécé

We started on the island of Itaparica, darkly outlined on the horizon on the opposite side of the bay and visible from most parts of Salvador. I had visited it once before with the ravishing Katia and could remember there was a small hotel in the village where the boat landed, plenty of empty beaches, and not much else. We had a contact, a Mother of the Saints called Dona Cécé, too poor to have her own cult house but who, so it appeared, operated from home down one of the side streets. A visit to the island and a chat to Dona Cécé might be fruitful and lead to a long-lasting relationship. We went across the water on a *saveiro*, a wooden high-masted boat which in those days was a very common sight, carrying to different ports around the bay a wide range of goods from building materials to sacks of rice and beans. It was relatively simple to get a lift for a few pennies. On arrival we jumped over the side up to our waists in water holding our small bag above our heads and waded ashore feeling that we were on the verge of making an exciting discovery. If she turned out to be friendly and welcoming we would find somewhere to live nearby and spend some months learning what we could and observing her at work.

Our arrival caused quite a stir. We were instantly surrounded by children wanting to carry our bag. Faces appeared at windows and small groups gathered to stare as we tried to get our bearings. I asked somebody for directions to Dona Cécé's house. There was a stirring and two or three children broke into a run and disappeared around the corner. We waited feeling conspicuously white and smartly dressed (only tee shirts and shorts but clearly of much better quality) next to these people who wore no shoes and had thick crusts of skin on the soles of their feet. They asked if we were *gringos*, a slightly deprecating term for *americanos*, and when we told them we had in fact come from Scotland which was miles from America, they didn't really understand. The staring was most disconcerting, but most of these people had never even visited Salvador across the bay, and having two white strangers in foreign garb in their midst was quite an event.

The children sped back round the corner and panted and stared. Then a tall black man with thin white hair and an engaging smile that revealed a flash of silver grabbed us warmly by the hand and told us to follow him.

'Call me Dadí', he said, and off we went with a large following that got larger as we progressed round the corner and down the street.

The houses on either side were all of one storey with tiled roofs and a window on each side of the door. The windows had no glass but slatted shutters that opened inwards. Every house seemed to have a 'fridge and a television and old tins with plants in them on the road outside. Paintwork was cracked and peeling but the general effect was very pleasing to the eye. Dona Cécé's house was no different to the rest: one room inside the front door, two small windowless bedrooms beyond, a corrugated plastic shelter over the cramped back yard which served as a kitchen. She was in the front room, flanked by her three children on either side and half a dozen neighbours who wanted a closer look at us. The gazelle-like daughters, Naomi Campbell look-alikes, but so much more beautiful and without the slightest hint of a pout, went to make coffee. In the meantime we had another exchange about America and Scotland, tried unsuccessfully to explain why we had no children (why should lack of money be a good reason when all *gringos* appear to have so much?), and answered endless questions from Jorge, the twelve-year-old son about what it was like to be in an aeroplane. When the coffee came it was mixed with *farofa*, finely ground manioc flour that sits heavily on the stomach and reduces hunger pangs. Gradually the room emptied and soon we had Cécé, the children and Dadí to ourselves.

There was an instant rapport. Cécé soon perceived that our work could only do good. Her life ambition was to put aside enough money to buy or build her own cult house but Itaparica was a poor place, and the inhabitants had no work or money so she was forced to charge the lowest rates for her services. A book about her and her work, however, could train the eyes of the world on her predicament and some Samaritan might just help by providing sufficient cash. Dadí, not her husband, but a close family friend who was very much of a father figure to the children, had two or three houses in the village which he tried, though without much success, to rent to the very few tourists who came visiting from the mainland. One would easily convert into a small cult house but the financial margins were too close for him to make the final gesture. After all, what would he and his large, extended family live on?

We took the cue and asked if we could view the smallest house. It was in an adjacent street with houses down just one side and a wide area of waste ground in front with a blue oil drum that served as a dustbin for everyone in the vicinity, far enough away from the front door not to be a nuisance. It stood out from the neighbouring houses because it was taller and had a first floor but in every other respect it was smaller than everyone else's. One slatted window to the right of the door as you went in; enough room for a rickety table and two rickety wooden chairs; a small recess for an ancient gas cooker with a grimy sink and tap to one side. Through a dirty curtain were a rudimentary shower and basin. A back door led to a tiny yard with high walls on all sides. From behind one of them came the distinct gobble of a turkey, a fine plump bird that would feed a large family for days. Up a steep stair was the bedroom with a double bed, a view through the window to the oil drum, and above our heads to the underside of the roof tiles. The heat up there was terrific but he assured us that at night it was relatively cool. He quoted a rent which we considered very high, but he said it was the same that he charged any tourists who might come for a week or two. There was no way he could understand the benefit of a long let and a subsequent drop in the rent. If we paid him the full amount he would provide a 'fridge, something we knew instantly we would not be able to be without. Deal done. We'd arrive the following morning.

17

Itaparica

It was predictably difficult getting our three ungainly bags from the quayside to the deck of the *saveiro* without falling through the gaping gap into the filthy waters below, and none of the crew seemed able or willing to help. Passengers on this service looked after themselves. There would be a mighty problem at the other end too when we had to wade the last few metres through the choppy water and up to the sandy beach carrying our belongings above our heads. The crossing was just like a passage out of Moby Dick with the billowing rust-coloured sail smacking and heaving, and all the wood and ropes creaking. Down below where we had gone to get out of the sun, water streamed in through cracks and holes in dire need of caulking but nobody seemed to mind. As we made ourselves as comfortable as we could sprawling on coarse sacks of grain we felt like the intrepid hero and heroine of a nineteenth century novel being transported to a distant, unknown land. The two or three-man crew kept themselves very much to themselves struggling silently with the ungainly rudder as I rehearsed how best to ask them to lend a hand with our bags when we arrived. If the typewriter and tape-recorder got a ducking we would, as they say at sea, be well and truly sunk. But in the end it wasn't as bad as we had feared. Rosie was able to manhandle the bags over the side onto my head and I made three trips to and fro whilst the surly crew impatiently drummed their fingers. It was later, as we sat at our rickety table, wet shorts drying in the yard, that we heard the honk of a ship and discovered that there was a modern link with the mainland in the form of a daily ferry. This was diesel-driven and made of steel, and much more sophisticated than the *saveiro* in that it allowed its passengers to disembark on a new concrete jetty, but we wouldn't have missed our significantly less comfortable trip on the creaking *saveiro* for anything.

The ferry arrived daily at 5 pm and everyone flocked to meet it. For a quarter of an hour there was hubbub and bustle. The postbag was first off and the man in charge sifted through all the letters, called out some names and distributed a number of them before cycling away. This scene had all the makings of García Márquez's *No One Writes To The Colonel* where happiness and fulfilment depend on whether or not a long-awaited letter is in the bag. Those without letters sat patiently on bollards hoping for better luck the following day. Families noisily foregathered with handcarts and wheelbarrows for loading goods that had been ordered in advance from shops in the city: plastic-clad 'fridges, tools, pots and pans, and crates of live chicks. Disembarking passengers usually looked a bit green and seasick for islanders displayed an extraordinary

Itaparica Island bus.

knack of becoming violently ill as soon as the ferry put to sea. The slightest roll or movement had them huddling in corners and vomiting over the side. The island bus, an ancient green and red contraption with wooden window frames and a split windscreen, always met the boat then lumbered off down the road belching diesel fumes and rolling from side to side, its roof-rack piled high with luggage. The crowds that had gathered so excitedly earlier on gradually dispersed like ants at the onset of night and the village slowly grew stiller and quieter until it regained once more its normal somnolence.

We settled into a routine. Every two weeks we went to the mainland to stock up in supermarkets. Yes, there were shops on the island: plain wooden huts with flaps over the window opening upwards, but they always had poor produce and small stocks. The butcher's shop was another of these huts with uncovered meat hanging from the ceiling or lying on a makeshift shelf outside the window, and there were flies everywhere. Meat could be bought in three different qualities: first, second or third. First quality were the best cuts but they had been visited by just as many flies as the other two. In fact, the third quality was probably less fly prone than the other two because it was heaped up at the back of the hut and the more discerning ensured that their portion came from the relatively protected off-cuts inside the pile. A friend of ours in Salvador once upset his maid by instructing her to get first quality meat for his dog, to which she retorted that in her family they always ate third quality. Permanently rancid butter in a five litre red tin could be bought loose at the bar but with the heat it was always virtually liquid and was well nigh impossible to get home in one piece. Sometimes there was bread. On the mainland, however, we could find everything we wanted so we stuffed our backpacks with heavy tins and bottles and carried the lighter things in tall brown paper bags provided by the supermarket. On the first occasion when we got back to our house we undid all the wrappers and plastic trays and put them in the paper sacks outside our door for me to take across to the oil drum when it was cooler. They weren't there an hour or so later because someone had stolen them. We learned there was a market on the island for second-hand paper bags which were carefully repaired with a needle and thread then put back in circulation. If we bought anything at an island shop and asked for a bag it was usually one of these.

In spite of the significant poverty on the island there was one outstanding state funded facility: a spanking new library building with a good collection of books, opened recently by the Governor Juracy de Magalhães with a smart plaque commemorating the event just by the entrance. It wasn't used very much and we heard mutterings from some people that you can't eat books so what's the point. Close by was the school, a solidly built edifice with grass growing through the cracks of the paving stones outside. Although we went past it often enough we saw and heard precious few signs of life. There were always clusters of children playing outside or not doing very much with their time as we went on our daily rounds so I suspect that attendance was poor. We never met the teacher, which is odd, considering we were the only Europeans, apart from the gloomy Englishman who ran the hotel, to have stayed on the island for any length of time.

The gloomy Englishman took no interest whatsoever in us but he seemed to do quite good business, particularly at weekends when people came over from the mainland for a change of scene. There was a veranda with armchairs which was his excuse for charging too much for a bottle of beer so we tended to go to the bar in the village where we were immediately the centre of attention. Word would go out that we were sitting outside in the street on the only two bright red plastic chairs, courtesy of Coca Cola, and people would come and, quite unashamedly, stand and stare. They no doubt thought that spending a few pence on beer was utmost profligacy, a sentiment which began to mean more and more to us as our own funds started to dwindle alarmingly. From the start one bottle of beer did for the two of us. The beer, a well-known Brazilian brand, was brewed with onions and every now and again you got the taste at the back of your mouth.

The island doctor was called Dr. Halley since he had

been born on 20 April 1910, the date of the last sighting of the comet. A small, gentle, quiet, moustachioed man, he can't have made much of a living treating the island sick who, despite his rock-bottom charges, found the cult houses cheaper and, perhaps in some instances, more effective.

Raimunda, seven children by seven different fathers, had never consulted the doctor in her life. She did odd jobs (mainly laundry) for odd people in order to feed her growing family. She was tough and resilient and it came as no surprise to discover that her *orishá* was *Yansan*, goddess of the thunderbolt and patroness of firemen. None of her menfolk could have been a fireman, incidentally, as there was the most rudimentary of fire services on the island consisting of a few red hose pipes coiled up near some hydrants. We employed her for just a few pence per week to do our laundry. There was an ulterior motive: she knew everybody, was a fund of knowledge about children's songs, rhymes and games, and she dabbled in the things that interested us so was able to introduce us to the woman at the head of a leading local cult house. Our washing never got very clean and it soon acquired a lingering, unpleasant background smell. We discovered why when we saw her tackling a pile of laundry in a dubious-looking ditch on the outskirts of the village, then spreading the clothes out on the ground and on bushes to dry. We were warned of the dangers of this: if a lizard scampered across the clothes we would suffer from *cobreiro* (shingles). All her other customers had suffered from it. We had been warned. The Grundig tape recorder was hard on batteries and Raimunda taught us how to open them and sprinkle the contents around the house to get rid of ants. It never worked for us so Raimunda took them off our hands and used them at home.

Drinking water was delivered every Thursday by an obdurate donkey staggering under the weight of two blue barrels on both sides of its saddle. We tipped the contents of each into a large earthenware pot in the kitchen. Water for the tank in the bathroom was piped from outside but was only turned on sporadically so we had to remember before going out for the day to make sure the kitchen sink taps were turned off. The tiny water tank was above our heads in the shower and was hardly enough for the two of us to wash so we had to use cups of drinking water to rinse off the soap and finish washing.

Loading obdurate donkeys with water, Itaparica.

One morning we were woken by angry shouts from the direction of the house directly behind ours. Most noises filtered through the open tiled roof but this was loud and very disconcerting. There were footsteps in the street and the sound of people running. Someone banged on our door, not the sort of bang that invites you to open up, but a brusque and unfriendly bang accompanied by sinister mutterings and more hurried footsteps. Our neighbour's plump turkey had been stolen from the yard and the easiest access was through our house and over our back wall. Naturally we denied all knowledge of this and tried to reassure them that we hadn't allowed anybody in to our house to facilitate the committing of the felony. But they refused to believe us and for some time the atmosphere was extremely ugly. Fortunately for us, Dadí was asked to mediate and after a while tempers cooled but it threw a gloomy shadow over the next few days and caused much bitterness and resentment among some of our closest neighbours. We had by then begun to lose quite a bit of weight as our meagre funds didn't stretch to one square meal a day, so no doubt they considered we had a very good motive. The irony, though we didn't dare breathe this to a soul, was that we certainly did have a motive and would have given anything to be able to cook and consume such a fine beast. We dribbled at the thought and despised and loathed the thief with the same intensity as the bird's unhappy and luckless owners who doubtless dribbled too.

Once we were visited by a beggar, a courteous man with a stick and a pronounced limp, who wanted something to eat. Apart from dried beans and rice which he couldn't have eaten we had nothing to hand apart from a cucumber in the fridge. When he touched it his eyes lit up and he said 'It's so wonderfully cold' then limped away holding it to his brow. He never came by again.

18

A god and a devil

Every morning we emerged from our front door, observed how the blue oil drum had been rifled by scavengers who were nightly in search of our rubbish, withstood the unremitting stares of neighbours at windows or doors, and walked the length of Cécé's street towards her house at the bottom. Rosie went with the daughters into one of the bedrooms to write down the words of rhymes and songs, while I sat with Cécé. At first I found this very unproductive because I didn't know enough about the subject to know what questions to ask, and for the first few days at least she had no customers. She was wonderfully cooperative in so many respects. I asked her about the trance state, how easy or difficult it was for her to enter it, and did she have total control over her body while she was in it. Could she, for example, return to normal if she wanted to? Her response was a little unnerving. She sat at the table and stared fixedly at the wall in front of her. Ten seconds later her shoulders hunched and she swayed back and forth, back and forth, then introduced herself to me as *Ogun*, her dark eyes staring with great intensity into mine. She muttered a few words in Yoruba which at the time were totally incomprehensible to me and a few moments later returned to normal. The whole experience can't have taken longer than a few minutes. She conducted all her consultations in trance and referred to *Ogun* as her 'lord', the 'owner' of her head. It was *Ogun* who healed, advised and prayed. She was the humble medium who knew at an early age that she was destined to be a Mother of the Saints and had done months of training in a cult house on the mainland.

Dona Cécé in trance

I learned an enormous amount from her. She talked me through the properties of over a hundred herbs, which *orishá* controlled them and what they were used for. Lavender, for example, is controlled by the two goddesses *Oxun* and *Yemanjá* who love all sweet-smelling substances; it is used primarily to fumigate a newly born baby and all the clothing worn by the baby and its mother during the first seven days after the birth; when soaked in water and tipped over the head it will also attract good forces; it must be picked before sunset - the picker should bow, gently clap his hands three times and say '*Dá licença*' (with your permission).

This gentle respect for plants extended to everything she did. Whenever one of her patients fell into trance she would welcome the *orishá* in Yoruba and sing his chants while holding the patient's hand and cupping the nape of the neck to ease the shaking. At all times she touched, squeezed an arm, reassured with a hug and generously gave of herself. After some months she called us her spiritual children and smilingly explained how our own *orishás* (*Oxun* – Rosie; *Oxossi* – me) were a fine match and that our marriage would last for ever. We were so impressed by this that we asked an artist we met in Salvador who specialised in the naïve style to do us a small painting of *Oxun* and *Oxossi*, the one dependent on the other, and it now occupies a central location in our house. Over the ensuing years Cécé has been proved right.

The Devil and all his works must not be talked about inside the house so she took me outside into the street to tell me about *Exú*. He is an *orishá* with a difference. The early slaves soon saw an affinity between him and the Devil but whereas the Devil is regarded by Christians as totally evil and devoid of good, *Exú* will always, if properly treated, work hard for the common good. All ceremonies and acts of healing must be preceded by a small propitiatory sacrifice exclusively for him for he is a jealous god and will disrupt proceedings if he is not given pride of place in the pecking order. He is essentially more demoniacal than diabolical, a trickster with a sense of humour who can and will turn nasty if he doesn't get his way. Small representations of him, usually a small phallic-shaped mound of clay, stand at a door or a cross-roads willing to guard and protect if properly catered for, or to destroy and hinder if ignored. Depending on the seriousness of the occasion an offering is always left for him: a spoonful of beans and rice at one extreme, a sacrificed animal at the other. In a corner of Cécé's yard ('Never allow him under your roof. Never mention him in the house. Never') was one such mound and the offerings were changed daily. 'Strong' herbs, particularly those with a sting, belong to *Exú* and can be used for good purposes, but when picked with the left hand can only be used for evil.

'What would happen', I asked, 'if you didn't make an offering to him first'?

'He would force the other *orishá* away, enter the medium himself and thrash his arms around, hitting people, breaking things, and it's very difficult to get rid of him when he's like that'.

Blood offering to Exú.

19

Dona Alice

Raimunda introduced us to Dona Alice, a fearsome-looking Mother of the Saints at the head of a proper cult house on the edge of the village. The thing that first struck us about her was that, although she had slight negroid characteristics, her skin was white yet she had been born and bred on the island. Her whiteness in this black and *mulatto* community was odd as we thought we were examining the evolution of an African religion but she was the offspring of a union some generations back between a white master and a female slave. Her house was no bigger than a bungalow and it had a spacious covered terrace in front where there were benches for people to sit, a separate area for drums and a door into the house from which cult members emerged dressed in the clothes associated with their *orishá*. Alice was very good to us too by allowing us to record and film throughout and we were given pride of place on the front bench which on the one hand was wonderful for the camera and tape recorder, but on the other did not permit us to slip away before the formal end of the proceedings. Evening sessions got underway at about 8 pm with the drums beating out all the different rhythms and didn't finish till about four in the morning. We thought that common courtesy demanded we should be active participants accompanying the drums throughout with clapping so we always had quite sore palms by the time we fell into our bed. We went to this cult house twice a week for some months and by the time we had finished were able to sing all the chants and stamp all the rhythms in the shower, much to the delight of passers-by.

It doesn't take long at the beginning of the evening's entertainment for one or two people in the audience to fall into trance, their inner memory responding to the familiar beat. Dona Alice appears, resplendent in the yellow robes of *Oxun*, her many gold trinkets jangling as she advances towards the medium. Again, with considerable respect (after all she is dealing with a god), she embraces, soothes the frantic shakings and swaying of the head, then leads the medium to a seat at the front. Soon the door opens and a dozen or so men and women, all part of the cult house hierarchy, emerge wearing the costume of their *orishá*. They form a circle and move slowly round and round in time to the beat of the drums. The beat grows louder and louder until it is thumping and knocking inside your rib cage while all the mediums move their bodies in accordance with their god's rôle in the pantheon:

Ogun beating open a path with his sword; *Yansan* effortlessly brushing aside difficulties; *Xango* wielding his axe; *Omolú* stooped and hobbling like the sick old man he is. At this stage they are play acting, mediums re-enacting their gods' doings as recounted in the myths. But suddenly the mood changes. One after the other they fall into their trances giving great screeches and thrashing their heads back and forth.

Alice, also in trance but more in control, welcomes each god and goddess as they arrive and calms the mediums down until they can resume their dance no longer as ordinary men and women but as Yoruba deities.

The gods begin to dance.

And so the evening continues, and the dancing and the clapping are interminable, and there is no break. Three hours have passed, the door opens again and out come women bearing aluminium pots and paper plates. It is time for the gods to eat: *vatapá*, fish or prawn mixed with coconut milk and oil; *carurú*, pounded dried prawn mixed with okra into a sticky glue (not a favourite of mine). These are the two main cult dishes but there are plenty of others. Various onlookers now approach and whisper their requests to Alice who in turn whispers to the gods. She passes their advice back: which herbs to take and when in order to cure them of their ills; what substances and herbs to place in the fumigator; how to deal with an errant wife or husband.

It is only when the gods choose to leave that the rest of us feel we can. The costumes are soaked with sweat and bear the odd *vatapá* food stain; the mediums are exhausted and ask us all how it went for they have no recollection of anything. There is one bright side to massive island unemployment: none of these people will need to face an employer in a few hours' time but they can stay in bed and get the sleep they

The gods descend.

badly need after so many hours of physical movement. Some, however, are mothers who scoop up their children from the floor and go home to snatch two or three hours' sleep before the baby demands his first feed. It seems so tough on all the participants, but when we ask them about it they say that, although physically exhausted, they feel revived and refreshed after emerging from their trance, like an athlete emerging from the gym after a work-out. It is at this stage, if any of the audience were ill at the start, that they begin to feel well again. Children are present throughout, gradually falling asleep as the long evening draws on, but they soak up the rhythms and observe their parents and neighbours worshipping the gods in their own way. When their time comes they look upon it as a natural transition like the first day at school. For them, falling into trance and bearing the burden of a deity is something that adults do, and they aspire to it from an early age.

Dona Alice (right) as Oxun.

20

Gnawing hunger

Round about this time we each wrote a long letter to Douglas outlining how we were getting on and what sort of material we were collecting. It took us a long time to prepare what to send him and as we summarised our findings we were filled with worry about whether or not what we were collecting could have any place in formal academic study. We were observing all these extraordinary practices and recording them dutifully on our index cards, but was this enough to qualify eventually for a doctorate? We needed reassurance yet we feared he might dismiss our research to date and advise us to follow another path. Five weeks later his reply arrived. We had expected prolonged notes, suggestions as to which areas to concentrate on, which to abandon altogether. What we got was one sentence on a post card showing the St. Andrews Abbey ruins incongruously looming out of a Scotch mist:

'You appear to be wallowing in a rich stew of stuff'.

Thanks Douglas. We'll take that as a yes then, and carry on as before.

Exhilarating though our lives were on the island we suffered a lot from island fever and needed regular breaks to keep sane so our shopping trips to Salvador across the bay soon turned into overnight stays. The ferry was a very small boat with room for only thirty or so passengers and a large area behind the bow for luggage and merchandise, but it was quite modern, made of plate steel and freshly painted so we felt quite safe. Other passengers, however, didn't and a wail went up as soon as the boat started to behave like most small boats in a choppy sea, and the sea was usually choppy. On bad days we were soaked with spray and had to put up with a great deal of sickness on all sides. The Captain must have noted the dour looks on our faces because he invited us to sit on plusher seats four steps up in the wheelhouse and we maintained this privileged upgrade until the day we left the island. We still had to pick our way in sandals across the slimy deck in order to disembark but our journey was a hundredfold more comfortable. On arrival we went straight to the flat of an old friend in the Bank, showered with unlimited water and lay on a proper bed without mosquitoes or hot humid air reverberating off the roof tiles.

Salvador was a charming and romantic city of organised chaos. There was a plethora of crumbling colonial buildings and a different baroque church round every corner. The church of St. Francis, the saint who, like St. Roche, gave all his considerable fortune to the poor, was lined with gold that glinted in the wan light stealing through the coloured windows, a powerful symbol of colonial riches. Outside, to complete the ironic reversal, were filthy and wretched beggars attempting to steal the hearts of visitors leaving the church, dazzled by the sight of so much wealth within. Another fine church stood at the top of a flight of stone steps and had recently been the setting for a scene in a Hollywood film.

The ostentatious wealth of Salvador's churches didn't only contrast with the ugly and upsetting poverty of the beggars outside. Although we never knew poverty like many of the beggars, or indeed our close friend Cécé herself on the island, we were beginning to feel the pinch as our meagre funds ran out and we found ourselves forced to rely more and more heavily on Rosie's small grant. My Brazilian scholarship, despite many expensive 'phone calls to various offices in Brasília, never materialised, and, as we feared, our small capital sum that we had sent over after selling our car hadn't lasted long. We did our sums time and again in a vain attempt to drum up more money than we actually had, but in more realistic moments it boiled down to so much per week that simply couldn't be exceeded. To overspend now would result in our having to abandon the rest of our plans, and that would require us to give up our research and go back to the UK empty handed, no job and a lot of explaining to do regarding the yawning gap on our CVs.

It was always cheaper to take the ferry to the mainland and scour the supermarkets for the cheapest food than to remain on the island and pay island prices. But the food we got was of very low quality. Black beans and rice were staples for the poor so our diet consisted mainly of that with the occasional plantain banana, tomato or pepper. It doesn't sound too bad but we could only afford small quantities and were always ravenously hungry. So much for the romance of poverty. We bought the poorest quality beans and spent hours separating the beans from the bits of grit before cooking them. The worst thing by far was going out with friends in Salvador to gleaming restaurants for dinner, lying about having already eaten our dinner, then gazing longingly at the copious dishes of food as our companions tucked in. They never finished what was on their plates, and we were too proud to ask, so a lot of what we could have had went back to the kitchens. We lost a great deal of weight and as we got thinner our stomachs shrank and demanded less at mealtimes, but hunger stole back soon after. Being hungry with no prospect of satiation puts you in a sound position to appreciate true poverty, and we certainly did that. We learned a great deal during this period which in retrospect we wouldn't have missed, but it was very hard.

A small tax rebate in the form of an Inland Revenue cheque for around twenty pounds arrived in the post but the Bank's iniquitous charges to convert this into local currency were such that we would have precious little change at the end of the transaction, so I promptly sent it back to Messrs Coutts & Co instructing them to credit it to my account. Harold Wilson was still in power at the time and my Bank manager, never a great fan of the Socialist Party, replied to my letter with the memorable words: 'You will be relieved to learn that Her Majesty's Government have honoured their draft'. Lying beneath the mosquito net in our sweltering little room digesting yet again a frugal meal of rice and beans, we cared not a fig for Her distant Majesty's Government, but the tone and total Englishness of the reply made us quite nostalgic.

We were still much, much better off than many of those

around us, however. Cécé told us she often went for a whole week consuming nothing but coffee with a spoonful of manioc flour so that her own children could have solid food, and yet every evening she watched a soap on the TV about people living in a sumptuous flat in Rio agonising over whether it would be better for their daughter to marry the ambitious, dull, straight-up-and-down lawyer with a fat salary or the bearded outdoor man styling himself on Mellors but with a comparatively small income and living the good life on a not so remote paradisiacal island just an hour and a half's drive from Rio. Their predicament was a million miles away from Cécé's but she knew precisely which husband the daughter should choose.

There were reminders of extreme wealth and utter poverty everywhere you looked. The red light district contained nothing but glorious colonial buildings harping back to an age of plenty but now in an advanced state of dilapidation with weeds growing out of the guttering and black mildewed stains on the façades. Through the open doors and windows were tantalising glimpses of stucco work and mouldings and the original wide boards still on the floors. Not so tantalising was the sight of thin young girls and women, hollow cheeked with big staring eyes, sprawled on the steps, touting for business.

Vivaldo, a short, rotund, neatly-bearded Professor of Anthropology at the University was interested in our work and we spent many hours together deciding the next way forward. In the absence of Douglas we hugely respected his advice and through him made a number of contacts who proved invaluable. One of his sidelines was to head the Salvador equivalent of the National Trust and he showed us his renovation plans for the colonial areas of the city. The ruling military dictatorship felt strongly about supporting the preservation of the national heritage and made it easy for him to find the funding necessary for this daunting project. There seemed to be a lot of money in the kitty so he was able to insist on the finest possible standards restoring, and thankfully not replacing, many of the original doors, plaster work and floorboards. He showed us round a distinctly pleasing building, the showpiece of the project that had recently been completed. All the tiny details, including the interior and exterior colour schemes had been properly researched and executed by first class artisans. Whenever a building was too run down or worm eaten, and sadly there were plenty of those, the façade was preserved and the inside rebuilt from new.

It was Vivaldo who suggested we should visit Professor Edelweiss, a retired academic living in a house facing the sea, with a collection of books that might interest us. The books started at the front door and lined the walls of every room. The Professor's study was on the landing and he sat at a desk facing you as you came up the stairs. Mild mannered, quietly spoken, he caught us out then taught us the correct pronunciation of his favourite English author Robert Southey (South-y as in north-y, not Suthy as in soap suds). He gave us a guided tour and we were delighted to discover an enormously impressive collection of anthropology books, rare studies by researchers the world over of Afro-Brazilian rites and rituals that we would at some stage have to read and mention in our work. They were all together in the same room and we were welcome to come as often as we wished to consult them.

We decided to take a two or three week break from

the island. Had we not discovered this library we would have had to spend a great deal of time at the British Museum which, despite being a copyright library supposedly with a copy of every book ever published, might not have had some of the more obscure works published only in Brazil. He was impressed by our tenacity and arranged with the housekeeper to keep us supplied with a steady stream of coffee provided we took special care not to spill a drop. Biscuits weren't allowed, but he watched us, quite rightly, like a lynx when the coffee was poured in cups that were then placed next to his precious books. As we talked we learned that he had left the entire collection to the University library on condition that it remained as it was and was never split up.

21

Cult of the dead

Vivaldo knew we wanted an introduction to the cult of the dead on Itaparica. Very few outsiders had witnessed it and the cult leaders were known to guard their secrets jealously. He would do what he could but could promise nothing. The days went by and then, without any warning, we were to meet him again outside the *Modêlo* market with its stalls of herbs and magic potions. He introduced us to two brothers, six-foot-six men who were so black you could see the blue of the sky reflecting off their skin. Vivaldo was nervous and treated them with the utmost deference. One of them had a basket of yellow chillis on his head and insisted we took a bite. This was indeed an experience, 'the name everyone gives to their mistakes', as Oscar would have it, and our mouths burned and dribbled while we endeavoured, with a crick in our necks, to explain our purpose. They weren't happy. They said nobody visited them and they would prefer it to stay like that. But we persisted and, after we had given our assurance that we would make no recordings and take no photographs, they relented. They would meet us late at night and lead us up a secret path through the forest to the clearing where the cult took place. We were to speak to no-one and leave by the same path as soon as the meeting finished.

This was very exciting news, but it was a blow that they had struck such a hard bargain forbidding photographs and tape recordings. For a while we toyed with the idea of taking the tape recorder hidden under our food in a bag but rejected this through fear of what might happen if it was discovered, and we certainly didn't want to be subjected to yellow-chilli torture or pick any sort of fight with those two brawny six-foot-sixers. They were making a rare exception for us so the decent thing was to play in accordance with the rules.

The meeting place was Mar Grande, a very small village consisting of a cluster of fishermen's houses on the west side of the island from which were spectacular views across the bay to Salvador. The two brothers in complete silence led us out of the village and along the road for a few hundred yards, then we turned inland along a path that soon began to climb steeply. We got one or two views of Salvador winking and shimmering across the sea and then we were plunged back into the utter darkness of the forest. There was no moon so seeing our way was a problem as the path was criss-crossed with tree roots and very treacherous in places. It would have been easier had we been wearing 'sensible' shoes instead of the flimsy sandals which, in that heat, were the only things we ever wore on our feet. The inevitable happened. Rosie caught her foot under a root and twisted her ankle badly so she couldn't walk. We thought the whole expedition was scuppered as both brawny brothers were impatient to get on. In the end they explained that all we needed to do was continue to follow the path (provided of course we could see it in the pitch black) until it emerged into a large clearing where the ceremony was to take place. We waited and waited rubbing the offending ankle in a bid to bring it back to life. Whole families went on past us talking in hushed tones. We thought we could hear the murmur of voices not very far above us, so encouraged by this and in great pain, Rosie limped the last few yards then we both sank gratefully to the floor of the clearing and looked around.

There was a large crowd, larger than any gathering of people we had seen before on the island. Everyone was sitting on the ground, children careering around excitedly, babies squealing and demanding attention. In front of us some twenty yards away were two old sheds facing each other, each about the size of a free-standing garage. The spirits of the dead were due to emerge from these later, so we gathered from those around us. One or two candles in jam jars cast an eerie light giving added height to the trees towering above the clearing. The drums started at about ten o'clock sounding quieter than normal because they were farther away. A man had already shooed people from the front leaving a wide strip free for the spirits to move in. We had become quite adept at recognising the main rhythms for the leading *orishás* but soon knew these rhythms to be different. The spirits that were shortly to appear were not going to be the Yoruba deities that we had so often witnessed at Dona Alice's cult house. As the drum beats pounded I was put in mind of an article I had read in Professor Edelweiss's library: Yoruba is a tonal language and a skilful drummer can make the drums copy some of the sounds of the spoken word, so what we were hearing really was a serious effort to communicate verbally with the spirit world. When they finally emerged from the wooden huts they wouldn't of course be non-corporeal spirits in the strict sense of the term, but mediums incorporating the spirits of the deceased. The cult existed exclusively on Itaparica because it was the only sizeable place in this part of Brazil where the sun set over the sea, a crucial detail in coastal West African death rituals.

At last a hush spread over the crowd and wayward children were brought into line. We sat uncomfortably on the ground straining our eyes in the poor light. When the spirits finally emerged there were about a dozen in all dressed in long white raffia robes with elaborate headgear that completely covered the face, probably to preserve the anonymity of the mediums. Two were inordinately tall in comparison with the rest and we assumed these were the brothers who had escorted us here. One looked like *Omolú*, moving with difficulty and wearing a mask to hide facial sores, but he could equally have been a representation of extreme old age and decrepitude. They moved painfully round and round in a circle the drums meanwhile beating louder and faster and so it continued for what seemed like an age. There were some mutterings in the crowd and children were forced to look at the spectacle which, if I am to be frank, was mildly disappointing. It would have been better if we could have seen more clearly but the ever-watchful organisers frowned on those that tried to sit closer to the action.

When food for the spirits was served we all took that as a sign, so picnics were opened and spread out, then the corporeal and the spiritual ate their fill. The children drifted off to sleep, and who could blame them? Conversations about everyday subjects struck up, as they strike up around hospital beds, and the spirits, like the patients propped up on pillows, were left to doze. There was a little more dancing, if you can call their laborious movements dancing, and then, as the spirits sought refuge again inside their sheds, the audience's willing suspension of disbelief was switched off like a light and they surged towards the path. As we hobbled down feeling our way in the dark we held up those behind who called to us to get a move on and by the time we hit the road and said our good-byes we had left the spirit world firmly behind us. We had to wait two hours for the ancient island bus to take us the few miles back to our village.

22

Raimunda

One whole corner of Raimunda's front room was given over to a shrine in honour of *Yansan* with a picture of St. Barbara at the top, red plastic flowers in red pots, oil burning in red glass containers, a few smooth stones (probably in lieu of real stone axe heads), one or two pots of water containing reddish leaves, and a bowl for food that normally was changed every day.

Located as it was in the main room of the house through which everyone had to pass in order to reach the front door, the shrine, like a Greek or Russian ikon, played a central rôle. Visitors pressed their palms together and made a slight bow. Raimunda's seven children took no notice, as you might expect, preferring to leave all the reverence to the grown-ups.

In these fragile societies where people have a firm and unshakeable belief in the spirit world the spirits themselves are given a hard time if things do not turn out as expected.

Whenever a small favour wasn't granted Raimunda withheld a candle or a food offering saying out loud: 'Sorry, but if you're too busy to look after me you can go without for a day or two, then you'll know what it's like'. Putting all your faith in the spirits' ability to look after you and protect you from harm is a great comfort in a harsh world provided the everyday vicissitudes remain bland and harmless. Raimunda, a formidable chatterbox in company, continued the banter when alone with *Yansan* in her own house, an illiterate spiritual equivalent of 'Dear Diary' where the diary is the silent recipient of all the day's news. But when the Prince of Darkness unleashed his dreadful forces *Yansan* retreated into the background and only re-emerged when the terrible initial crisis was over.

Raimunda (right): shrine to Yansan.

Raimunda's fifth child, a five-year-old bundle of energy with laughter in his eyes and an unruly shock of curly brown hair, was alone in the kitchen where the beans for lunch were boiling on the gas stove. The insatiable curiosity of the young was his downfall for the pan came down over his head inflicting first degree burns all over his upper body. There was little that could be done on the island with burns of such severity so preparations were hastily made to get him on the ferry which fortunately had not yet left, and then to a hospital where he could be treated. Raimunda, in a state of utter panic, ran round her friends, including us, begging for coins to finance not just the ferry but the taxi afterwards and a possible prolonged stay in Salvador. The little boy might have pulled through had there been a paramedic team on the island, or a helicopter to gain precious moments, but the lumbering ferry took one hour to get there and the taxi got stuck in traffic. By the time he arrived at the hospital there was no hope and all his mother could do was sit by his bed and watch his life ebb away.

She was sunk in gloom. It wasn't just the stabbing grief and gnawing sense of guilt, but now there was the additional expense of bringing the body back and paying for a burial. For the first few days regular customers held back their laundry in the mistaken belief she didn't want to be bothered by such a thing at such a time, and this made her income plummet. Of course we all rallied round. Cécé recommended herbal baths, remedies for depression and a number of sessions with fumigation to dispel the ill wind that had come her way. It was some weeks before she was anything like her old self but she was a woman of considerable resilience and strength, and regarded this tragedy as an evil that poor people are destined to encounter regularly during their lives. There's not much the gods can do if, through parental carelessness, a child is exposed to danger, so *Yansan*'s reputation as protector and comforter remained untarnished. St. Barbara was soon back in favour with a lighted oil lamp revealing the miraculous breach in the wall of her tower, and casting a dim glow over the other curious objects that made up the shrine.

23

Spiritism

Raimunda went regularly (perhaps more regularly after the death of her child) to a Spiritist session run by Dona Alice every Thursday. It was of great interest to us for we were assured that illnesses were cured during the session for no charge. This was entirely different from the *Candomblé* meetings that took place on the terrace outside her house at weekends during which participants with an illness were expected to make a payment towards the general running expenses of the cult house. Spiritists practised healing and all manner of charitable acts for no charge at all, which accounted for their popularity.

In Spiritism, illness is believed to be caused by the actions of disembodied spirits floating around in the ether, getting up to no good. Those spirits with a more positive outlook and who are free from all evil inclinations work through mediums to transmit good energy that flows like a 'fluid' or an 'electric current' in to the patient thereby overcoming the illness and making him well. The Yoruba pantheon of deities have no rôle to play here: the spiritist mediums embody spirits of the departed, often the spirits of those who worked as medical doctors in real life, and they give advice about how to treat the symptoms.

Spiritism was first developed in France by Léon Hippolyte Dénisart Rivail (1804-69) who published his works under the pseudonym Allan Kardec that was given him by his spirit guide. The long-established African tradition of relying on the intercession of an *orishá* incorporated in a medium was the principal reason why Spiritism became so immediately popular in Brazil. We were particularly fortunate on Itaparica to have met Dona Alice who had one foot firmly planted in both camps. On the one hand she cured through the intercession of Yoruba deities; on the other she relied on the spirits of men and women with no overt connection to the African tradition but with the power to cure.

Spiritists whenever possible wear white. There is no chanting, certainly no drums, no dancing, no ritual food. Alice scaled everything down to the bare essentials: a room three metres by three with a large table surrounded by six or eight chairs; other chairs on which participants and onlookers may sit; the windows thrown open so people outside can have a view of the proceedings. At the beginning she asked for all the requests to be placed in writing on the table. Illiterate patients had to ask the literate to write for them. She browsed through the lot, sifting them into some order, then called for silence. It took no more than a few seconds for the first spirits to appear, the mediums flinging their heads back and forth and speaking in the spirit's voice, low tones if a man, higher tones if a woman.

194

Alice then read out the requests and the spirits would reply stating what specific herbs should be taken, or indeed, which medicines should be obtained from chemists on the mainland. Each patient in turn then came to the table, sat and held hands with the mediums on either side so that the beneficial forces could pass through the body and cleanse it.

We saw nothing spectacular, no crutches cast aside and life-long cripples begin to walk, but people talked openly a day or so later about how much better they felt and how the symptoms had subsided or, in many cases, disappeared. Psychosomatic? Probably a good dose of that, but these people had little or no money so the spirit session played a crucial part in controlling general sickness levels on the island where western medical attention was relatively expensive. The power of suggestion brought by a group of committed believers achieved high levels of success and cost absolutely nothing.

'I am going to Rio to visit Teresinha's father', said Alice to all of us assembled in the tiny room one Thursday in the deep male voice of the spirit she was embodying. Teresinha hadn't heard from her father for some time and needed to know if something was wrong. Alice laid her head on the table, closed her eyes, and appeared to fall into a deep sleep. In fact, 'she' did none of these things. It was the male spirit within her that absconded and remained absent for half an hour. Whilst Alice stayed completely motionless slumped at the head of the table, other mediums conducted the rest of the day's business, stating which concoctions should be taken and at what time, and forming a circle to permit the 'electric current' to flow through the patient and cleanse him. All went smoothly until, without any warning, Alice sat up straight and emitted a low growl.

'I am at his apartment. I am opening the door. There's a small table on the right with papers and a vase'.

Teresinha shouted:

'Yes, you're at the right flat. That's his table with letters and a vase on it'.

'I am going through the bedroom door, the one on the right, and I see the bed by the window'.

'Yes, that's the bedroom, and that's just where his bed is', shouted Teresinha, tears now streaming down her face.

'Your father is ill. Very ill. It can't be long now. Take the bus and visit him'.

Cries of anguish from Teresinha and a bit of a commotion as she fought her way across the room and ran back to her house.

She went to Rio, a journey of two days in a bumpy bus with hard, unforgiving seats, and somehow managed to cross the city without a hitch to the familiar building where her father lay dying. Twenty minutes later, his hand in hers, he was no more. His daughter declared to all on her return that the spirit alone made this possible and that she would have been eternally consumed by guilt if she had not been able to be with him during his last moments.

Cynics might well say at this point: most flats have a small table just inside the front door; it's a fifty fifty chance that the bedroom is on the left or the right as you go in; beds tend to be by the window, and what exactly does 'by the window' mean anyway?

Cynics are quite right to take this coolly objective view but the people present on that steaming Thursday afternoon who witnessed the proceedings would take issue with them.

We all knew Teresinha's predicament: her letters had remained unanswered; her father had no 'phone so 'phoning was impossible; she had ruled out a telegram in case he was too ill to answer it. Asking the spirit to make the trip for her and to ascertain precisely what was going on was the only option. None of us grouped around Alice's table that day was prepared to doubt for one second that her spirit had indeed made the journey and returned with advice as to how Teresinha must proceed if she was to see her father before he died.

24

Cachoeira

The imperceptible signs of the seasons, some gusts of cooler air, white horses leaping across the bay, more brown leaves than usual drifting down the village street, all served as reminders that our time on the island was drawing to a close. We had arrived with little or no knowledge of Brazil's African heritage but now we could greet Cécé in three-hundred-year-old ritual Yoruba, recite the qualities of dozens of different herbs, tap with our fingers the drum rhythms that summoned the gods, recognise them as they descended towards the faithful, and have an educated guess at what the patients would be prescribed.

We knew too, after a very short acquaintance, which *orishá* controlled whoever we met, and which combinations of *orishá* would lead to the happiest and longest enduring relationships. We saw clearly the link between this and the ancient science of Astrology where the position of the planets at the moment of birth dictates the direction which the baby will follow, or informs the astrologer how best to interpret a person's future. We also knew that the Christian God was not part of any of this, that the links between African deities and Christian saints were tenuous and had originally been established by men and women in fetters desperate to keep their ancient beliefs alive.

On Itaparica much of what we had witnessed was very remarkable: people with little or no income at peace with themselves, sure in the knowledge that their gods and spirits (a veritable Communion of Saints) existed for the common good, spoke and advised through mediums, taught reverence for plants and ritual food, and constantly reinforced the belief that the spirit world and the tangible, standing close together side by side, often overlap.

Our departure engendered even more kindness from the people with whom we had lived for several months and who had willingly, without any thought of profit, answered a myriad of questions and told us everything they knew. Cécé was genuinely upset and dreaded the chasm of loneliness that would open up once we had left. She knew we would probably not return to the island in her life time so this was a good-bye that had all the abrupt finality of death.

'You are my children', she said. 'I will always worry about you and think of you. May *Oxossi* and *Oxun* protect you'.

On our last evening we were to go to her house and eat with all the family. She protested when we arrived laden with food:

'I wanted to share one meal with you before you left and now you've brought enough for days'.

Her two gazelle-like daughters had spruced up the house. The two wiry sons had shifted the worn plastic sofa to make more room. There was a familiar single plastic flower, duly dusted down, in a cup and our names written large on scraps of paper where we were to sit. It was a joyful, loving occasion with a steady stream of neighbours and friends who wanted to say good-bye. Dalva, who had spent hours with Rosie singing children's ditties and explaining the intricacies of local games, spent the evening sobbing in a corner. The television was on throughout as nothing was so important as to warrant missing an episode of the favourite soap, so we ate our beans and manioc flour with all the drama of unrequited love blubbing on the screen, and plenty of 'Oos' and 'Ahhs' from the live audience round the table. We handed over our gifts, trinkets of little value, that nevertheless gave immense pleasure and would be treasured for years. Cécé stood at her door as we walked back home, a crowd of children at our heels, and when we turned and waved, those black piercing all-knowing eyes were awash with tears. We were saddened too, having to abandon people who had become such friends, and were worried that Cécé would feel bound to answer our letters and spend on one stamp for Europe what she would normally put towards a week's food. But we had promised faithfully to stay in touch.

In the morning we stowed our cumbersome bags on the deck and sat with everybody else fearing that eager fingers might undo the straps and remove things if we left them unattended and went to join the Captain for the last time on the bridge. Our last ferry trip across the bay was punctured by the usual squeals of the islanders as the boat pitched and tossed from

Farewell dinner with Dona Cécé.

one white horse to another, foam rising high and boiling on the deck. Soon the island was a long dark line on the horizon with, clearly visible, the hill on which we had communed with the spirits of the dead as Rosie's sprained ankle throbbed with pain. We felt decidedly nostalgic for our little house and the abandoned dog we had befriended who struggled to survive on the scraps thrown into the blue oil drum opposite our front door.

At the squeak of rubber on metal we were back on the mainland struggling with our absurd bags to a rendez-vous with Vivaldo who had promised to find us free accommodation in Cachoeira and would be handing us a key. Cachoeira was an unknown that we had chosen at random for its location on the river Paraguaçú, one of the furthest towns from Salvador on the other side of the gaping bay with its many inlets.

As it happened, he handed us two keys and declared we could take our pick between a tumbledown mansion that had dilapidated furniture and a rudimentary kitchen, or a recently restored seventeenth century ten bedroomed town house that was as bare and as full of echoes as an empty aircraft hangar. If we decided on the latter we would have to buy sticks of furniture and some means of cooking and preparing food.

'So in this instance', he said, 'beggars can be choosers'.

He said it with a twinkle in his eye but he knew, as indeed did we, that the only option was the crumbling mansion as our ever-meagre resources could never stretch to furnishing a small palace, however tempting that might be.

We discussed our work and he nodded in approval, but he seemed to think that now that we had a profound understanding of the structure of African beliefs, we needed more evidence of cures, and the more spectacular the better. Had we heard of Zé Arigó, the ice cream maker in a small town in the middle of the Brazilian interior and many miles away from Salvador, who operated in trance with a penknife to remove gross tumours and then miraculously stopped the haemorrhaging? Yes, we had, but American anthropologists had already filmed him at work and we had to err always on the side of originality. Douglas' warning to avoid plagiarism at all costs and to be primarily concerned with new work that no-one had recorded before still rang loud in our ears. Maybe in Cachoeira, a town that had more difficult access to Salvador than Itaparica, there might be a more sophisticated cult house that operated primarily as a health centre for the townsfolk and for those who lived deep in the interior. He helped as much as he could and gave us the name of a teacher, Professor Roberto, who would certainly be able to point us in the right direction.

Armed with two keys and a verbal introduction, and fighting our achingly heavy bags, we struggled towards a bus park on one side of a square in the upper town that sent rusty, dented buses at erratic times far into the interior. We had a long time to wait for there was not a great demand for buses to Cachoeira and the timetable reflected this. One or two women sat on low chairs at the kerb, gloriously bedecked in white turbans and long flowing white robes (*Oxalá*, we said knowingly to each other). Before them were pans of sizzling *dendê* oil cooking *acarajé*, a spicy doughnut served with an eye-wateringly hot pepper sauce.

Manuel Querino, one of Brazil's first food writers, said in 1923 in his book *A Arte Culinária na Bahia* (*The Culinary Art of Bahia*) 'Bahia stands for superiority and excellence in Brazilian culinary art and is highly esteemed because the African element with its spicy seasoning and exotic ingredients completely transformed the culinary traditions of Portugal which resulted in a tasty and uniquely Brazilian product pleasing to the most demanding palate'. Not surprisingly these daughters of *Oxalá* were doing good business, wrapping their wares in banana leaves for travellers to take with them on the buses. Men with a penknife peeled oranges in one strip starting at the top and going down to the bottom without a break, then displayed the spring-shaped peel from their baskets as they went from one queue to another selling their fruit. For some odd reason (maybe an obscure fashion accessory?) they all wore on their heads, like a generous-sized skull cap, the bright yellow net bags which originally contained the oranges. In the tarmac of the road surface where the buses drew up was a

Cooking acarajé, Salvador.

veritable Milky Way of crown caps that had been stamped into the soft tar over the years and now gleamed like so many stars at our feet.

When it finally arrived our bus hardly inspired confidence. Side spoilers had long since disappeared leaving rusting holes where the rivets had been; bumpers were dented and awry; a tyre displayed an alarming knuckle duster set of pressure bumps, and re-treads looked ready to unpeel at any moment. We were to become quite familiar with this bus over the coming months and soon learned to avoid the rear off-side wheel arch where the weary suspension sent jolting spasms through the floor and into adjoining seats. It was least uncomfortable directly behind the driver but the constant reminders that he wasn't totally concentrating on the job (drumming fingers, head bobbing in time to the endless cacophony blaring from a dusty ghetto blaster propped precariously on the front shelf and obscuring part of his view) filled us with fear that this might be our last journey ever. Where the gear lever reached the floor there was a very good view of the roller coaster road surface, and from east to west across the windscreen stretched, tentacle-like, a crack with a chip the size of a florin at the level of the driver's eye.

We examined with a good deal of curiosity the motley set of passengers as they alighted: a man with spurs wearing a heavy leather hat held together with thongs and carrying a gaudy cartoon magazine; two or three women on a long journey with suitcases tightly wrapped in calico and crudely stitched; a group of raucous young girls on their first trip to the city drenched in heady scent, dark lips an incongruous red, clutching cheap plastic handbags. These people told us nothing more than what we might have guessed: Cachoeira was going to be similar in all sorts of ways to Itaparica, bigger and somewhat more cosmopolitan, and perhaps not as easy a place in which to make friends quickly. We boarded the bone-shaking bus with a touch of apprehension as to what the immediate future might bring.

Having left the untidy suburbs behind us we soon plunged into deep forest then emerged on to a gently rolling plateau with miles and miles of sugar plantations on either side and the occasional glimpse of lush bluey-green tobacco leaves. The road bumped and twisted from one cluster of houses to another where we picked up and dropped passengers at their request. Where the tarmac had washed away were blood red gashes of soil, a reminder that not so long ago it would have taken us the best part of a day to cover the same distance by dirt road. It was difficult to imagine our route following the shape of the bay but far enough inland not to permit a glimpse of the sea. If you were to hover in a helicopter high above the Bay of All The Saints you would see jagged fingers of water piercing the coastline with a number of rivers flowing into their tips. The Paraguaçú is navigable by sea-going vessels until they reach Cachoeira whose very name translates into English as 'rapids'. There are islands, the biggest of which by far being Itaparica, and inland, usually on the rivers, a number of sizeable market towns. Until comparatively recently (1980s) these towns were supplied from Salvador mainly by the gracious, heavy, workhorse *saveiro* boats that transported everything from piles of cement and heaps of tiles to 'fridges, washing machines and spices.

From your helicopter you may just make out our long, winding narrow road from Salvador skirting the bay in an anti-clockwise sweep ending in São Felix on the west bank of the Paraguaçú, overlooking the larger and more dominant Cachoeira on the east bank, a tropical reconfiguration of Budapest where Buda and Pest wink at each other on opposite sides of the river. But whereas Buda is joined to Pest by a graceful sweeping iron and stone bridge, an exact replica of the one crossing the Thames at Marlow, São Felix and Cachoeira are linked by a crude angular construction with railway sleepers in lieu of a proper road surface that knock and bump whenever a vehicle chooses to cross it.

This thirty mile wide, sixty mile long strip of land around the bay is exceptionally fertile and well watered, and has a soil type particularly suited to the cultivation of sugar and tobacco. In the early colonial days it was a centre of large landholdings owned by a white rural aristocracy and founded on slavery.

207

Sugar was introduced from Madeira and the first African slaves began to be imported in 1538 to work on the plantations. By 1587 there were already forty seven sugar plantations and mills. If you look very carefully from your helicopter you will see still standing in clusters of giant mangoes and tall palms the remains of some of these buildings with the tell-tale stump of the mill chimney. Next to them, but far enough away so that the refined aristocrats could not be disturbed by the nightly throb of drumming, the single storey row of buildings, home to the slaves without whom the land could not be cleared or the ever-abundant sugar and tobacco harvests brought in.

After processing, the goods were despatched to Salvador by boat, then loaded into merchant ships for the long Atlantic crossing. Sugar loaves wrapped in blue paper conically shaped like Rio's aptly named Sugar Loaf mountain, and fine cedar wood cigar boxes with neat little brass catches were all destined for the butlers' pantries of the homes of Europe's richest and most influential families. Fabulous fortunes were made and embarrassingly rich extravaganzas were indulged in. The very wealthy even sent their linen for laundering in Lisbon's clean fresh water, a round trip of three months. Stocks of linen had to be large indeed to keep a whole family clothed in that climate without the benefit of air conditioning.

Named after the very first high-earning export, the dyewood that glowed red like a *brasa*, or 'ember,' and grew in vast quantities near the coast, Brazil never knew a period like this again when sugar and tobacco commanded the highest prices and sweetened and permeated the finest drawing rooms. Not one of the European consumers paused to consider how both commodities had been produced in a far-off land, the crack of the whip being the only noise heard above the gentle murmuring of the breeze through the brittle canes and lush tobacco leaves, but they no doubt prayed in a mellow stone church to a Christian God who lauded tolerance and understanding throughout His kingdom, and they gave renewed thanks for the continuing safe arrival of the merchants' storm-tossed ships.

These musings killed time as we bumped and squeaked our way, shutting our ears to the ghastly background music, gripping the greasy aluminium bar to stop falling off our seats. Our first glimpse of Cachoeira was of weathered roof tiles in the southern European style resting on old walls bathed in the golden light of late afternoon. There were no outskirts – just a sudden transition from rural to urban, the first houses of just one floor soon becoming gracious three storey town houses in need of a good lick of paint but all with a peculiar old world charm.

We might have arrived at a small town in Portugal in the 1930s before the onset of cheap and ugly building to house a growing population. Towards the centre the streets broadened and on our left, through occasional gaps in the houses, we could see the shimmering oleaginous surface of the river.

Our luggage, as usual, caused quite a stir as it fell clumsily from our hands down the three steps on to the pavement. Professor Roberto was well known and soon we were following an eager group down the twisting back streets towards tall trees and the beginning of the countryside. Again we cursed our bags that took all enjoyment out of our first excursion into our new home town where the distances were so much greater. The straps dug in to our shoulders and we kept tripping over the

River Paraguaçú, Cachoeira.

third bag that was slung between us banging in to our legs.

The welcome from Roberto dispelled all the misgivings we may have had in Salvador about plunging into a new and unknown place. He was thin and wiry with a wide grin that revealed perfect white teeth. His thinness he explained was due exclusively to the macrobiotic diet which he and his family followed very assiduously. Macrobiotic was a new word to us but it seemed to suggest strict vegetarianism judging by the raised beds in his back garden that were brimming with gleaming vegetables of every description emerging from well tilled and composted soil. We drank filtered water ('tea and coffee dehydrate') and learned how we were slowly poisoning ourselves eating food full of pollutants.

'You must be careful', he said, 'only to eat food that is home grown, no meat, and an occasional bit of fish.'

We didn't mention that we were so permanently hungry nowadays that we would willingly eat anything alive or dead that may be placed before us. Unfortunately, his hospitality ended at the glass of water, suitably cleansing but with no nourishment, and we were soon off again, armed with instructions about how to find the dilapidated mansion.

We were to cross the railway sleeper bridge to São Felix, then look for an overgrown path on our right that ascended through shrubs and bushes and eventually arrived at a small wooden gate. We missed the path which, as we later discovered, was literally where the bridge touched the bank, and walked on into São Felix dragging our bags with us, suffering by now from heat exhaustion and greater hunger than usual since we hadn't eaten properly since the previous night at Cécé's house where the fare had hardly been sustaining.

The path was steeper than we would have wished and right from the outset our ascent was a Herculean struggle. We daren't leave the by now much hated third bag at the foot of the path and go and fetch it later for fear that it might prove too tempting to one of the many children that had stayed with us since our arrival on the bus. So clutching it with both arms I led the way up through the dense branches and brambles unable to put out a steadying hand or to pull myself up by an overhanging branch.

What had seemed at street level to be the distant barking of a couple of over-excited dogs now turned into a mad furore which got louder and louder with every step. When at last we reached the peeling gate held shut by a loop of rusty wire we could see them clearly. They were chained to the railing of the lower veranda, straining away from us, white saliva glistening on their muzzles. Our raising the loop and pushing open the gate caught their attention for a moment but instead of transferring their anger to us they turned and continued their frenzied barking in the opposite direction, hackles up, tails stiff, saliva now dripping in great globules onto the planked floor. It was as if someone were standing close by, taunting them with a bone, for every few seconds the barking turned into a whine of fierce frustration as the tongues attempted just one lick only to be forced back into the mouth by the terrible pull of the chain.

We stood transfixed, unable to comprehend what it was that made them behave like this. The end of the veranda was twenty feet beyond them then it turned and continued its way around the ground floor of the house. Having finally dumped my bags, I went round the other way to see if there was someone there, but there was nobody. The most alarming thing was that when I finally emerged round the corner on the dogs' side, they continued their terrifying barking, not at me who had just emerged out of the blue from behind the corner, but at the invisible thing or person that was standing just inches from their slavering jaws.

Hardened though we were by several months of greeting gods and spirits in the flesh, nothing had prepared us for being in the presence of a spiritual force that could not be seen. Were we witnessing such a thing? We knew that dogs bayed the moon but this dreadful barking was aimed at a considerable, albeit invisible threat. Was there a poltergeist here, and might that be why this crumbling mansion with its wide views over the roofscapes of Cachoeira and São Felix, had stayed uninhabited for years? The very thought shamed us. There would be another explanation when we met the person who would come at some stage to feed and water the dogs but, even if there were an explanation, would it be sufficient to dispel our conviction that someone or something invisible to us was taunting them from very close up?

It was with some relief that we discovered the small key Vivaldo had given us didn't fit the rusty lock on the front door because this gave us a cast iron excuse for not living in the house after all. We were far too exhausted to negotiate the path again so, despite our gnawing hunger, we propped ourselves up against the wall and tried to ignore the din the dogs were still making. Something was maddening them, that was for sure, and once or twice, we nodded off as an exhausted soldier might nod off in the thick of battle with his back against the dug-out wall. But sleep brought no rest and the dogs continued, hoarser now, to harass their unknown tormentor. We stayed there some hours in a vain attempt to shake off our growing fear that the dogs were somehow trying to urge us to stay away for our own good, but at three o'clock with numb limbs and a hollow feeling in our stomachs that wasn't only hunger, we found ourselves back on the steep path slithering down to the street. Cachoeira was as still as the grave while we remained huddled on a bench waiting for dawn. No noise came from across the river. We convinced ourselves the dogs had finally settled now that they knew we were no longer in danger. We never went back.

A screech of parrot and a flash of crimson, blue and green met our arrival some time later at Dona Maura's guest house. The long-tailed parrot, whose *Guaraní* name *arara* was onomatopoeically spot on, was caged in a corner of the yard with the stripped branch of a tree for its perch and at its feet in black oily mud slept an armadillo, its colour and style like an early prototype of the Citroen 2CV with reinforcing corrugations on the bonnet.

'We keep it for the cockroaches', remarked Dona Maura. 'You won't find any here. The smell puts them off'.

Fortunately, we were far enough away from the slumbering beast to put this to the test, but it is true that during our stay we saw no cockroaches. The absence of cockroaches, however, in no way compensated for the boisterous parrot who screeched '*arara*' every two or three minutes between dawn and dusk with the exception of a twenty minute break for lunch when it cracked Brazil nuts in its vice-like beak for its main course and tackled six inches of unstripped sugar cane for pudding. As we gazed nervously at this feat of strength it fixed us with its dry yellow eye as if to say: 'One step closer and I'll go for the throat'.

Our neat little room with its view over the yard (armadillo mercifully too low to be in our field of vision, although the ever restless *arara* regularly flew up into it as if searching for clues of our whereabouts) was a veritable haven of rest and comfort after the traumas of our first few hours in Cachoeira. The antiquated and noisy air conditioner hanging precariously out of the window managed to reduce the room temperature to thirty degrees Centigrade which surprisingly was quite a comfort. In the bathroom at the end of the corridor was an over-sized Edwardian-style shower head attached to the underside of an electric box, wires emerging from the top, missing the spurt of water by no more than an inch or two. When you opened the tap, the air conditioner cut out and every light in the house flickered and burned more dimly until

Making the acquaintance of an arara.

the tap was turned off. It would not have passed the least stringent of safety regulations but, provided you didn't fling your arms around and make too much of a splash, it was perfectly safe, although you did feel as you entered the plastic cabinet that you could be embarking on the last precious moments of your life.

Refreshed by a shower and a meal consisting of manioc flour (what else?) and a mud-tasting river fish with a cataract eye, we took our second key to the seventeenth century town house that stood in a row along one of the main thoroughfares in the centre of town. Directly opposite the front door was a bar, and further down the street a cinema built of wood with a wheelbarrow outside to which was attached a sandwich man's sandwich board for advertising the film. The house had the clean smell of wood preservative and fresh plaster with fine rooms on every floor but, as we had been told, there was nothing inside, no furniture or hangings to deaden the ring of our voices or footsteps as we prowled around wondering where we could set up home. We settled on a smallish room on the ground floor with views over the garden, an overgrown patch at the rear, and a bathroom complete with its own version of killer shower. Perhaps that nice Professor Roberto with the sparklingly clear drinking water would be able to help find a few sticks of furniture.

'You must devote the whole garden to vegetables', he said. 'Leave a corner free for your Tai Chi exercises. It's so nice having people here who appreciate these things'.

He gave us on long loan a couple of lightweight camp beds which, until we got the hang of them, we found impossible to lie down on without a serious collapse of the main supporting struts; a plastic table just big enough for our typewriter that had to be placed on the floor at meal times; a couple of folding chairs that, like the beds, had a tendency to fold when you least needed them to; an ancient saucepan and two thick white plates. We bought a camping gas cylinder with pan-holding attachment, a paper thin frying pan that just survived the five months we were there, two knives and two forks.

Self-denying monks in remote monasteries across miles of desert would probably welcome such lavish luxuries but we found the Spartan quality of our existence in Cachoeira very difficult to bear. There was nothing in the town to relieve the endless monotony of the simplest meals sticking to the bottom of the pan, no cheerful or lively place to go and soak up a bit of human warmth. The bar opposite our front door consisted of a large room lined with shelves bearing dozens of jars of sugar cane brandy in each of which was a different variety of snake. The owner gave small boys a penny for each live snake they brought him which he then inserted still living into the brandy of one of his jars. He swore that each snake variety had its own special taste and indeed, on the rare occasions when he had any customers, usually leather-clad cowboys from the interior who left their horses untethered in the street outside, the conversation got as close as you could get, given the confines of Cachoeira, to the lively chit chat of a Berry Brothers rare claret tasting. Further down the street was another bar called Night and Day in bright neon, but someone had thrown a stone through one side of the sign which now said Nig –y. Despite its name it was hardly ever open and clearly found the competition from the snake man too fierce.

Between the two bars stood the cinema, looking more like an elaborate garden shed than a cinema with a flight of wooden steps leading up to the front door. The sandwich boards in the wheelbarrow were re-pasted with posters every week then the barrow was pushed around town. All the films were American, dubbed, and mildly pornographic starring shapely, scantily-clad heroines seduced by Errol Flynn look-alikes with pencil-thin moustaches. The scantily-clad heroine occupied most of the two wheelbarrow posters which every week had a band across them saying '*O Gran*

Sexy'. Not surprisingly every film was a sell out. Queues would form an hour before the start and we could hear the excited chatter drifting in through our garden windows. Then at regular intervals during the showing, no doubt as some item of frilly clothing was removed, there would be a shattering roar of approval and we liked to imagine the entire wooden building swaying from side to side as whole rows of the audience stood to applaud. These animal-like roars were interspersed by the long, low wails of the snake barman's retarded son who sat on the kerb during opening hours swaying gently from side to side, groaning uncontrollably and snatching at unsuspecting passers-by.

The São Felix bank of the river could be seen whenever there was a gap in the houses on the Cachoeira side and the view was usually dominated by the tobacco factory, an imposing edifice dating back to the eighteenth century, largely abandoned since the advent of mechanisation. The façade was two storeys high, capped by handsome ceramic finials, and the wide windows, each equi-distant from the other, caught the sun at certain times during the day and gave the building a grand, almost palatial air. The pleasing symmetry of this view with mature palm trees in the background was reproduced on the inside of the lid of every cedar wood cigar box that left the factory. A shop window in Salvador displayed all the different qualities and sizes of cigar in their boxes with the lids propped up, and the immediately-recognisable coloured etching of the factory gave them all a seal of respectability.

Old men in white linen suits, black cigars clamped in

their mouths, strolled up and down, stopping occasionally to admire the elegant tobacco factory across the water while fanning themselves with battered panamas, nodding a greeting as we came and went, staring wistfully after the young who pushed past noisily in their haste to do not very much. On Saturday evenings cowboys came on horseback from the interior, faces the colour of hide, grasping intricately plaited leather whips. Ford Willys jeeps covered in mud and dust, diesel engines clanking and clouds of black smoke belching from the exhaust, parked in the street outside our door and disgorged men and women with calloused hands and voices used to shouting great distances. They went to the cinema then drank in the bars till the early hours when, with much honking of horns and over-decibelled farewells they returned to their lonely farms.

This was where we lived for several months, a period of hard work certainly but also one of isolation and loneliness, surrounded by people lacking in ambition, aimlessly living lives full of lost hopes and controlled frustration. Roberto was a kindred spirit and friend of sorts but he was too dogmatic and quirky to be with for longer than a few minutes. He was proud of his *Tupí Guaraní* Indian heritage and never tired of repeating with an inappropriately light-hearted broad grin his own version of Hamlet's mournful lament: '*Tupí* or not *Tupí*, that is the question', but his sense of humour and capacity for witty repartee stopped right there.

Family and friends, probably sensing from afar how isolated we felt, took to sending us tape letters which we slotted in to the Grundig. This was a great step forward but we found it almost impossible to reply. Neither of us was used to dictation (perhaps if I'd stayed in the Bank I would by now be very proficient at it) so our replies were verbal stumbles from one dreary point to another, and when we played them back we sounded like 1950s news readers, clipped, formal and terribly plummy. One tape from home had five minutes of Rusper parish church bells, a quintessentially English carillon that was interrupted by live expletives from the wooden cinema. After the bells, we were treated to the sizzling of the Sunday joint as it was taken out of the oven. We found that one very difficult to bear as by now we had eaten nothing but rice for weeks on end and our daily intake was enjoyed about as much as school semolina without the jam. If a slice of Baron with Yorkshire pudding could have materialised at that moment in our sparse room we'd have fallen on it like wolves. Another tape consisted of a dinner party with fine cutlery and glasses clinking above the sound of civilised English comments about the excellence of the food. But they had no idea what we were going through. We were too stubborn and proud to send a begging telegram, so silly in retrospect, but in a weird and warped way we wanted to see it through to the end without any reliance on anyone but ourselves. As the kilos melted away I punched holes in belts.

25

Dona Isaura

If we had had steatopygian characteristics we might have better withstood the daily ravages of hunger. '**Steatopygia:** *accumulation of large amounts of fat on the buttocks*' (OED), is a permanent characteristic of certain African tribes and is believed to aid survival in places where water and food are not abundant. Like the camel's humps, the swollen rump consists of deposits that the body can draw on in extreme circumstances.

Dona Isaura, well into her nineties, had distinct steatopygian characteristics which were clear for everyone to see because, unlike most nonogenarians, she spent her days, not dozing in a chair, but wandering down the street, talking to relatives and friends, playing energetically with great-grandchildren and great-great-grandchildren of which she had an ever-increasing number. Dona Isaura's steatopygia made her sway gently from side to side as she walked but even at her great age this did not cause her to lose her balance. She told us that when she had her babies she strapped them to the base of her spine taking the weight on her protruding buttocks, and that when she worked as a cleaner she would balance the bucket of water on the shelf of protruding flesh and proceed to wash the floor, dipping the sponge periodically in the water without having to straighten up first.

Originally from one of the Bushman tribes, her ancestors would have sailed past Itaparica full of dread at what lay in store when they finally docked after a long, arduous and filthy journey packed head to tail like sardines. Isaura herself remembered clearly working as a slave girl on a sugar plantation near Cachoeira until 1888, the year when slavery in Brazil was finally abolished. She recalled the long row of terraced cottages on the fringe of the estate where she lived with her parents and other slaves. Her masters treated them well and Isaura spent her days with the master's children whose French mother read stories and verses to them every day in French. As always happens, the favourite passages were re-told time and time again, and by a process of linguistic osmosis Isaura found herself able to recite whole passages off by heart without understanding a word herself.

Much to our delight and astonishment she could still rattle off poems and folk tales with all the panache of a native speaker although there were long passages that, over the course of time, had degenerated into gibberish.

We immediately recognised the key words *Maître corbeau ... arbre perché... fromage... renard... laisse tomber sa proie*, and on playing our tape over and over could just make out the rest of La Fontaine's *Le Corbeau et le Renard*, a classic from the first book of fables committed to memory by generations of French children to this day. She also sang in her old cracked voice a recognisable version of *Au clair de la lune, mon ami Pierrot...*, and as she sang she moved her head gently from side to side as French mothers do to keep the child's attention.

This direct link to Brazil's past as a slave trading nation we found distinctly attractive because she could only remember kindness during her years as a slave but sadly her memories of everyday details, her father's labour in the fields, her mother's work as a maid in the big house were gone for ever and, try though we might, we never prised anything more out of her. We would have liked a first-hand account of long nights of drumming and the appearance of Yoruba deities in their midst allowing them a few brief moments of liberty, but nothing was forthcoming. Either she chose not to expand on her past or the memory loss was genuine.

Few are the people, however, that have communed with an ex-slave who could remember the moment of liberation, her father lifting her high in the air shouting 'We're free, we're free', her mother watching in tears; an ex-slave who could recall, however imperfectly, bedtime stories and songs that were told and sung every evening as her father plodded wearily back from the sugar fields to his lodgings, cumbersome shackles on his ankles, and her mother spread out the linen for the dinner table in the big house dining room. Her story came to life every time we took the bus to and from Salvador past the dilapidated low-ceilinged slave quarters and the much grander abandoned buildings of the sugar barons just visible through the dense undergrowth that now surrounded them.

26

Carmen

In 1875, thirteen years before the joyful scenes of Brazil's slaves celebrating their hard-won liberty, the *Opéra Comique* in Paris staged the first performance of Bizet's *Carmen*. Those in the most expensive seats ate *pâtisserie* in the interval sweetened with Brazilian sugar and the gentlemen smoked Brazilian cigars hand-rolled by the ebony maids and matrons of Cachoeira. Bizet's beautiful gypsy woman Carmen, highly flirtatious and endowed, among other things, with a fiery temper, woos a soldier, then falls for a bullfighter, leaving the soldier so wracked with jealousy that he murders Carmen so no other man can enjoy her delights. Most productions feature an exotic heroine, red carnation clenched between dazzling white teeth which contrast so endearingly with her perfect southern Spanish olive complexion, with strong yet beautiful hands untarnished by long years of labour in the Sevilla tobacco factory where she rolls cigar after cigar while yearning wistfully for higher things.

The real Carmen we met in Cachoeira used to work in the tobacco factory overlooking the sluggish river, but unlike Bizet's Carmen, she was abandoned by her husband with five hungry children, and made redundant by the factory bosses as new machines spat out cigars and cigarettes a hundred times faster than the ladies could make them. She also lacked sex appeal and found it impossible to attract a new man. If she had found a carnation she would never have dreamed of gripping it between her teeth, flashing her eyes or playing hard to get, so her life without the support or income of a man, soon slipped into drudgery and extreme poverty.

Her ex-husband however, was not entirely evil because in his haste to cast aside his duties as husband and father he left her a house. As houses go, this was nothing special, with mud walls, two rooms and a flimsy, flaking front door, but it was just big enough to offer shelter for all the family. A small shrine to *Ogun* in the corner nearest the door always had a flame burning in a blue glass bowl, and just outside was a rusty tin holding an over-crowded spiky '*Ogun's* Sword' plant (*Sansevieria zeylanica*) which I tripped over several times during my stay in Cachoeira, the sharp leaves piercing my flesh which itched for days afterwards. The biggest asset was the garden, twice the width of the house, that stretched fifty metres down to the river bank. No one had worked in it for years and the jungle had taken over.

The children had beaten a narrow path down to the river which the family used as a bathroom suitably screened from the neighbours by the impenetrable vegetation on either side. With a regular income she might have been able to be relatively comfortable in such surroundings but she only managed to earn money piecemeal when odd jobs came her way so there were horribly wide gaps when, with no money, the family starved. *Ogun*'s light, however, burned without a break.

We had been inspired by Roberto's vegetable garden, a series of raised beds free of weeds, each producing such an abundant harvest that he and his wife only rarely needed to spend any money in a shop. Why not try to establish another vegetable patch in Carmen's garden so that within three weeks or so the family could start eating their own food? We would clear the area, buy some seeds and teach her the fundamentals: how to thin seedlings, the importance of weeding and watering every day. Later she could harvest her own seeds and become virtually self-sufficient. Carmen was excited by the idea and urged us on. Nobody else in her district planted vegetables so she would be the first and somehow this gave her a healthy touch of self-importance and might raise her status in the community.

Like many ideas it sounded feasible in theory so, armed with Roberto's forks and spades, and a well-worn, shiny, razor-sharp machete, we set to and spent a long, hot afternoon slashing and burning in true Amerindian style, feeling a glow every time Carmen came out, an infant on each hip, to plot progress. *Ogun* now had two flames burning in front of him, probably in anticipation of the free food that would soon be coming in the family's way.

We speared each seed packet with a twig and stuck it at the end of the row, all the time explaining what she should do over the coming weeks. To give them all some instant encouragement we had bought a well-established tomato vine in flower with tiny green tomatoes already showing where the flowers joined the stem. I attached it with string to an old chair leg, watered it in, then with hugs all round, and further exhortations about the importance of maintenance, we left them having sown one or two seeds of hope as well as all the others.

It was unfortunate that our departure led on to a three weeks' stay in Salvador working in Professor Edelweiss's library because when we finally returned to Cachoeira and went to see what we confidently expected would be a flourishing vegetable garden we met with a depressing scene. It had reverted to jungle and our carefully cleared and sown vegetable patch had disappeared from view.

'What happened?', we enquired forlornly of Carmen.

'I don't know. It just went like that all by itself. One minute it was as tidy as you left it; the next it was like this and far too overgrown for me or the children to clear it up. We're all fed up with it now so please don't bother any more with it'.

Our grandiose plans to teach a family to feed itself had suffered a fatal blow and we blamed ourselves for not having delayed our trip to Salvador for a few days. We could easily have done so because our time was our own to

Carmen.

organise as we pleased.

We yanked up a few weeds but the seedlings had been stifled by weeds and deprived of water so weren't worth salvaging. There was one slight glimmer on an otherwise very gloomy horizon: the chair leg to which I had tied the tomato vine had sprouted a couple of leaves but the vine was well and truly dead. It was as if we were the protagonists of another García Márquez novel urging the reader to abandon all links with reality. It is a fact that chair legs don't sprout when planted, but it is another fact that, being made of wood, there might just be the faintest possibility that they could. Reality and unreality in this instance had merged until the one became the other, and truth could reveal itself as stranger than fiction. We left the leg busily carving out a new life for itself, the fresh green leaves emerging from one of the original turner's grooves, standing as a symbol of what might have been achieved in this fecund spot.

When tragedy hit the family we were plunged once more into the midst of a friend's uncontrollable grief, rendered even worse by the lack of money to pay for proper help. Nine-year-old José had met with a similar fate to Raimunda's son: a boiling pan on the hob filled him with curiosity and when his mother was some fifty metres away behind the vegetation of the river bathroom, he strained to see what was cooking for supper and the contents of the pan spilled all over him. He was already in hospital when she came to see us wide-eyed and tearful, the other children at her skirts.

'He'll pull through if only I can feed him properly, but I've got no money'.

Even in those days hospital beds were available at no cost for serious cases but it was up to family or friends to provide the food. We were feeling the pinch ourselves more so than usual. The bill for our countless 'phone calls to far-flung Brasília in search of my grant was alarmingly high and the friend whose telephone we used urgently needed reimbursing. We had been eating nothing but rice and onions for some time in a desperate attempt to save some money to put towards the bill so when Carmen asked us for help there was a limit to what we could do. In the end we gave her what we would have spent on ourselves in a week with a promise of more in due course. The following day we saw her in the market holding a bag of six imported apples, an almost unheard of fruit in the Brazilian interior.

'I have spent all your money on these', she said, 'they'll make him better. They're imported'.

All we could do was dwell on the punishing curse of ignorance which, as we had just seen, won't be eradicated at a single stroke. First Carmen's lack of ambition with regard to the vegetable garden, and now these ridiculously expensive apples from Argentina were living proofs that it takes generations to change deeply rooted ideas and misconceptions. The poor continue to suffer in the meantime, trapped in a vicious circle from which they find it impossible to extricate themselves.

When the news of José's death broke we hurried round to her house and for the second time in as many months witnessed scenes that were hard to behold. Her face had lost its shine and for the first time we saw her steadfastness give way to a quiet and relentless sobbing. She sat with her remaining children around her clutching at her clothes. They were not squabbling and jostling as usual with all the exuberant energy of the young, but tearful and subdued, shocked by their mother's sadness, not understanding the full meaning of death and refusing to believe their brother would never return. Neighbours stood silently looking on. A woman dusted the shrine, joined her hands in respect and bowed to the picture of St. Anthony. Someone broke the silence and spoke of the relentless suffering of the poor. Why were they singled out? Where was the justice? Why did God abandon them and pour all His beneficence on those who didn't need it?

'*Senhor Ogun*, protect us'. And we all replied in a whisper:

'Blessed be the hour, oh my God, in which *Ogun* was born'.

27

Vicente

Over a glass of tepid and deeply-cleansing water Roberto told us of a man called Vicente who lived in the far reaches of the town in his cult house at the top of a steep hill. I went by myself in the morning asking directions at every corner for the *pai de santo* (father of the saints) called Vicente. Everyone knew him, which was a very good sign, and after scrutinising this thin lanky Englishman (in fact, they would certainly have assumed that I was an American), they put me on the right track. When the houses ran out and the road dwindled to a path with no dwellings on either side I became slightly anxious. Stories of foreigners straying into remote areas and then coming to no good abounded in Salvador and this was a fine abandoned place for an ambush with thick undergrowth on either side hiding no doubt armies of thugs. I eventually arrived at a black quagmire where a couple of pigs were picking over piles of accumulated rubbish and was directed to the top of the hill directly above the evil-smelling marsh which, to my dismay, I had to cross in my sandaled feet. Poor wooden and corrugated-iron housing patched with beaten tin cans lay on either side of the track, and men, women and children gathered at doors and windows to plot my slippery progress up to the top. When the track levelled out Vicente's house could be seen among clumps of shrubs and herbs, standing alone with a small, neatly swept courtyard in front, all the woodwork covered in gleaming white paint. The white flag on the roof declared its status in the community: this was the house of a man who worked with forces of good as opposed to forces of evil.

Vicente's cult house.

The house itself was modest with small rooms and a pleasant background smell of toasted thyme and rosemary. Vicente and I sat on plastic chairs while I stated what I was after. His face darkened and he said what I feared: that revealing his secrets could jeopardise his power as a healer. On the contrary, I argued back, knowing how hollow my arguments sounded, the publicity could add to his renown and prestige. He was not convinced. He had a steady stream of patients and didn't need publicity. We sat on and chatted, and then he said:

'At least you can speak the language. I had another American here some weeks ago but we couldn't understand each other so I sent him packing'.

'All I want to do', I said, 'is observe, tape record and take some photos'.

As soon as I said it I thought what a tall order that was but he seemed to have warmed to me and when I told him that I wasn't American but from a country miles away from America we began to get on very well indeed. After an hour or so he lifted my tee shirt and slapped me hard on my thin back.

'You are fat', he said, and I knew at that moment that I had won him over.

The rain came from nowhere and pelted down as only tropical rain can. Vicente's house loomed above me through the billowing trees so I turned hard right for shelter towards a front door. The owner, a wizened old man with white stubble on a jet black face, moved over to make room. He had in his hands a long pole that easily stretched out across the width of the track in front of us which he used to poke bits of rubbish that had flowed down to his level into the gushing rivulets of water which took them away from his space down to his neighbour's. And yes, coming from the neighbour's front door and from houses immediately beyond were other poles poking at rubbish ensuring its continued progress right down the hill to the bottom. My companion now emptied the dubious contents of a large tin can directly into a fast-flowing stream of water at the foot of his front door step. He had slopped out and now it was the turn of his untreated sewerage to start bobbing its way downwards.

'We do this whenever it rains', he said, 'so the water can take it away to the bottom of the track'.

'What about the neighbours lower down?', I asked. 'Surely they can't like it very much?'

'That's why we all have poles like this to help it on its way. As you might expect, there's a premium on houses like this one at the top of the hill'.

Poles right down the lane continued poking and teasing until at last the rain eased and the sun emerged from behind a cloud. I began my slithering descent down a spotless track knowing precisely what to expect when I reached the bottom. The pigs were busy at their work in the filthy quagmire while people came and went avoiding the worst by stepping adroitly from one tuft of grass to another. I went to Vicente's house daily for many weeks and was frequently caught out by the daily downpours but with time I thought no more about this novel way of disposing of sewerage. That is the trouble with poverty and its many attendant problems: the more you grow accustomed to it the more readily you push it to the back of your mind. It is all too easy to arrive at the stage where you ignore it altogether then, like its unfortunate victims, you begin to regard it as normal.

For the first two weeks I sat in a corner of Vicente's treatment room watching him treat minor ailments and prescribe herbal remedies. While there were slight variations between his methods and Cécé's, I learned nothing new. The patients that came and went behaved just like someone in a busy high street consulting the chemist for a bit of advice then purchasing a packet of medicine and going home. Here at Vicente's of course, the medicines were all based on herbs.

His cult house was quiet compared to Dona Alice's. There were never any sessions involving mediums attracting Yoruba gods, no drum rhythms, and Vicente himself, as far as I could initially ascertain, never went into trance. I began to think that maybe I wouldn't learn much new from him apart from the identification of a few more herbs but he assured me that if I waited I would be sure to see him perform a complex act of healing on a seriously ill person. He explained in some detail what I already knew: that illness is regarded as a force of evil that is best removed from the body by physical means (wiping, beating, washing, fumigating), all accompanied by chants and possibly animal sacrifice. He could not remember a single instance when he had been unsuccessful. So this was going to be worth waiting for.

When it happened for the first time it was dramatic and left my rational brain in something of a turmoil. We only noticed the horse when we heard the rustle of leaves and the sound of chomping. The man was not sitting astride it but was strapped to its back in the way in which corpses are transported in Cowboy and Indian films. There was a rope round his wrists that passed under the horse's belly and was tied to his ankles. We all thought the man must be dead for his head was to one side, his face swollen, pebbly and covered in pink blotches, and on first inspection he didn't appear to be breathing. His clothes seemed tight and a few sizes too small. It was a miracle that he had arrived at the right place because the horse had come totally by itself with no-one to lead it, a distance of forty miles. This was a detail I found impossible to accept: how could the horse have transported the man all that way without directions from a driver? Vicente assured me later that this was the man's first visit so his horse had not memorised a previous journey. All very odd and another example of the blurred distinctions between reality and unreality, truth and fiction, but I had to accept it as there was no other possible explanation.

We untied him then carried him with some difficulty because, as we moved towards the house, the body that looked so lifeless groaned with pain. Vicente cut his clothes to reveal swellings and pink blotches all over his body. The swellings were so bad that we could not create any space between his legs. This was a severe dose of elephantiasis characterised by gross enlargement of the limbs, torso and the head, and I thought the most sensible thing would be to get him to a hospital, and fast, but of course dared not mention this to Vicente. Normally, advanced stages of this condition are treated with chemotherapy or a selection of different drugs, but Vicente treated him over two days with chanting, fumigation and a herbal bath. When I say herbal bath I do not mean a bath in our sense of the word: no bath tub full of the essence of herbs which might indeed have had some effect, but a small recycled tin filled with dried herbs topped up with water, then poured over the head. The solution only comes into contact with the head and there is too little of it to reach other parts of the body. It is difficult to imagine that this herbal solution (as much as would fit in a small baked bean tin) could have anything more than a psychosomatic effect. And yet two days later after one such bath, and two fumigation sessions the gross swellings had gone and the man's face appeared normal. He got up from his bed, put on borrowed clothes, paid his bill, got on to his horse unassisted and rode away.

Somehow Vicente had managed to reduce the swelling and contribute sufficiently to the man's general sense of well-being enabling him literally to rise up and walk. I was the only one who couldn't believe my eyes. Vicente and his helpers had seen it all before, but only forty eight hours previously we had all thought he was dead.

Vicente's explanation was quite simple: he had invoked the assistance of *irmãos de luz* (brothers, or spirits, of light) who had passed through the patient's body cleaning up the evil forces that were making him ill. He had also invoked *caboclos*, the spirits of Indians who are believed to heal with the assistance of all the considerable forces associated with the jungle: powerful wild animals and the spirits that dwell in rivers and plants. It emerged that Vicente himself had after all been in a trance that was so controlled I hadn't noticed and it was the 'current' flowing from Vicente through to the patient that had done the trick. The power of this sort of healing, directed by the cult leader with fumigation and a herbal bath was there for all to see. It could not be explained by logic but that was no reason to suggest that it can't have happened at all. Indeed, I had witnessed it. Vicente's explanation, impossible to accept on one level, had to be accepted on another.

On one of our frequent trips to Salvador we had met a man who every Thursday laid hands on patients with advanced cancer and arrested the onward creep of the disease to the extent that none of them went on to die of it. The important variation in this case was that the man in question was not a cult leader but an ordinary member of the public in trance, allowing a 'current' to pass into all the patients and cleanse them. The experiences I was having raised so many issues: if this method of healing worked in Brazil why shouldn't it work elsewhere? The great French anthropologist Lévi-Strauss had already suggested that for such healing to work three things needed to operate at one and the same time: the patient had to believe that the healer could heal; the healer had to believe that he had the necessary power to heal; and the society in which both patient and healer lived also needed to believe that the healer could heal. The difficulty does not lie with the patient or healer but in coercing the vast majority of different societies fundamentally to change their deeply rooted practices and systems of belief. On the surface this is unrealistic but with so much at stake and a healthy measure of determination it need not prove impossible. The society, for example, need not be a random collection of different people living and working in the same area, but a select gathering of healers and their assistants working with patients towards a common goal in an enclosed environment – an environment not at all unlike a Brazilian cult house or Spiritist centre.

We were entering a new world governed, as some might say, by the power of mind over matter, but there was more to it than that. Somewhere there was a force, not yet properly understood, that had the power to heal, and we were observing it first hand. We had seen many minor ailments cured in similar ways, ailments that might have cured themselves in time, such as mild depression or sore backs. But serious diseases, usually only curable by western medicine with a wide array of specialist treatments at its disposal, were on an entirely different plane. On a political and social level there was little point in these people entreating their government to supply more doctors and build more hospitals if cult leaders such as Vicente, and indeed ordinary members of the public, could, at a fraction of the cost, cure people with advanced rare diseases such as elephantiasis so quickly and so successfully. My experiences were turning out to be deeply satisfying but at the same time they were very worrying on a personal level because no British academic, apart from Douglas himself, would be likely to believe what I was witnessing without solid scientific proof, and I was about to rely on a British academic from another university to read my work and, hopefully, award my Ph.D.

28

A doctor, a teacher and a lawyer

Two weeks later. A glint of sunlight off the windscreen, then the shiny car came to an abrupt halt outside our door with the scrunch of the handbrake and out stepped three smart women in their mid thirties checking that I was the man who Vicente had told them would conduct them to his house. The car owner was a doctor who had brought two of her patients for a curing session with Vicente but the odd thing was that the doctor herself was also going to be included in the ritual. All three suffered from migraine symptoms which the doctor had been unable to dispel with drugs currently on the market so they decided to join forces one weekend, drive from Salvador and consult the man whose reputation had spread to the capital. I was naturally intrigued by this development: a young medical doctor who had graduated from Medical School ten years previously, and two of her patients, one a teacher, the other a lawyer, had come to Vicente seeking a cure for persistent migraine.

'It's not simply a question of Physician, heal thyself', said the doctor as I steered their way through the streets to the track that led to Vicente's house. 'I have tried everything but we are all still suffering from regular splitting headaches'.

'How do you think Vicente can help?', I asked incredulously. At this point the conversation between a research student and three professional women, a doctor, a teacher and a lawyer, became surreal:

'There must be an evil influence, perhaps a disembodied spirit, stopping the usual medicines from working. That's why we're here.'

The others chipped in and agreed that after the ritual Vicente was about to perform they would all be fine. 'We believe the *irmãos de luz* (brothers of light i.e. good spirits) will make us better'.

'It's not the first time I've sent patients to see him', said the doctor. 'He's always worked wonders – literally. He prepares their bodies spiritually by expelling all evil so that my medicines work better'.

'In other words', I said, 'what we are about to see is some form of exorcism'.

'Exactly', they all chorused.

Vicente embraced them one by one, held their hands tightly and stood for a while looking into their eyes. Then he knelt down, drew a chalk circle on the floor and a number of five pointed stars ('Solomon's' stars'). The three women stood within the circle while Vicente went round and round them unwinding three new cotton reels until the women were cocooned in the thread. Then he cut the cotton with scissors to free them saying all the while:

'Cut away all obstacles, break down all the forces of witchcraft and sorcery with the power of the Holy Spirit, cutting, setting apart, annulling all the forces of evil which must be cut out of the bodies of these children so that good may surround them'.

In quick succession he 'wiped' the women symbolically with three raw eggs, three cigars, and three squares of plain black, red and white cloth, breaking the eggs and the cigars, and tearing the cloth afterwards, all the while reciting prayers specific to what he was doing: 'Wipe them clean...Break the evil...Tear the evil forces...Smoke them out'. Now he beat them hard with banana leaves, and took all the waste outside. He brought in a live cockerel and asked each woman to hold the beak close to her mouth and whisper into it what she hoped to achieve by having this ritual performed. Both the legs and wings were then broken whilst the cockerel was still alive and then its throat was cut with a knife. I was not allowed to witness the sacrifice but had to turn my back on it and switch off the tape-recorder. The last thing he did was sprinkle gunpowder on the floor around the circle, light it and stand well clear, shouting at the top of his voice:

'I am cleansing these bodies, removing all sorcery and evil in the name of all the *orishás*. I am leaving these bodies as clean as the Virgin Mary left the body of her Blessed Son. Jordan's current will sweep away all the evil that is in the bodies of these children. The whole current of the stars and of the waters, the current of the virgin jungle will sweep away all the evil. Evil, leave these bodies. These bodies belong to the Virgin Mary.'

There was not an explosion but a whoosh that enveloped all three in a cloud of smoke, a fitting and dramatic ending to a ritual where all the acts had been symbolic of enforced physical expulsion of an evil presence that was making the patients ill. None of the three writhed on the floor, thrashing her limbs; none shouted out with the voice of her tormentor, as might have happened in an orthodox Christian exorcism ceremony. As exorcisms go, this one had gone remarkably smoothly because an evil spirit is usually loath to leave a body where it has taken up lodging and the possessed person can suffer many traumas while the priest struggles to expel the forces of evil. Vicente was in trance throughout but he never showed it, and as he cleared up he said that all would now be well, that their tormentor had left and they would have no more headaches. On the way back to the car there was a quiet assurance about all three of them. Each seemed to know that from now on they would be better.

Three weeks later I bumped into the teacher in a busy street in Salvador. She was hurrying to a class so our conversation was brief and to the point. All was fine. None of them had suffered any further headaches. So here was another impressive performance by a man with no academic qualifications who lived up a muddy track in a small town miles away from the State capital. Three professional people on good salaries had driven into the interior for healing by a man in a trance who had physically driven away the evil forces that they believed were making them ill.

We could draw the obvious cynical conclusion: if you believe there is a devil within making you ill, then give it a good thrashing and it will go away. The three women certainly believed that a force none of them properly understood was causing them to suffer. But these were not the poor descendants of African slaves. All three were white and highly educated and yet all three had just been cleansed not only in the name of the Holy Spirit (perfectly acceptable in any Christian church), but in the name of all the *orishás*. Moreover, currents of water, 'currents' of the stars (by this I assume was meant the power of the heavenly bodies), the 'current' of the virgin jungle (all those hidden spiritual forces in the jungle) combined to expel the evil. If the successful outcome was psychosomatic we have to consider how a doctor, a teacher and a lawyer could possibly believe that Jordan's current, and all the other currents, were efficacious and that their headaches were caused by an evil presence inside them. At first sight this flies in the face of everything their education would have taught them.

On the other hand, why should this be a factor in determining whether or not they were acting rationally, and should reason necessarily enter into our motivation for actions and beliefs? Of course not. You can be as educated as you like, but in some corners of Brazil you believe in other powers because your parents believe, and all your family, friends and people around you believe. Lévi-Strauss's three important conditions as a pre-requisite to success had been achieved. Surely this is the story of Faith the world over. If you are brought up in a certain tradition you may faithfully follow the precepts of that tradition while relying on your rational mind to help you lead a rational life. There is nothing so unusual, therefore, about Brazilians leaving room in their rational mind for beliefs which to others may appear primitive or medieval. And they are in good company. Members of other religions also have beliefs which to others appear hardly credible, and Christianity has more than most.

Christians the world over occupy dominant and influential positions yet still have firm belief in the Virgin birth despite the fact that it defies rational analysis. Roman Catholics believe in transubstantiation, the process whereby bread and wine at Communion somehow are transformed into the body and blood of Christ. 'The body of Christ', says the priest as he distributes the sacred Host to the faithful, and yet how many of the faithful have paused to consider what this really means? A Catholic aunt of mine quite happily used to accept the priest saying in Latin at Communion 'Corpus Domini Nostri Jesu Christi', but she shrank back in horror when the English translation 'The Body of Christ' was introduced in the early sixties. The linguistic change had made her consider for the first time what receiving Communion truly implied.

I had read in the newspapers that when the hardliner General Garrastazu Médici was sworn in as President in 1969 he was swept away after the ceremony in his limousine, still wearing the presidential sash, to a back street in Brasília where he received the blessings of the *orishás* and *irmãos de luz*. Was it so incredible that such a man should have such beliefs? Not at all, because in Brazil the two can exist side by side perfectly happily and a belief in the power of African *orishás* does not necessarily demean the believer. On the contrary: the new President's willingness to broadcast his desire to link with Brazil's African heritage enhanced his standing among the poor who, in those days, regarded their poverty as a permanent state out of which they could never emerge, so his extreme right wing politics on the whole went unchallenged. With the glaring exception of a select band of freedom fighters, one of whom is now (2011) the country's new President, the majority of the population, the chronically poor, although opposed to Médici's *modus operandi*, meekly accepted that he was here to stay until the end of his term. The naïve assumption was that if the gods had accepted him, so should they. The richest cult houses in Salvador played host to the State Governor and several other thinking, rational people: teachers from the University and a famous contemporary novelist. The President was already in good company.

Vicente invoking the 'current' of the stars.

'Wiping' away the evil before sacrifice.

29

God is Brazilian

'*Deus é brasileiro*' (God is Brazilian). You overheard it in bars and restaurants, saw it on the TV, read it in the newspapers. It was adopted by Tourist Offices as the slogan for colour posters of the Iguaçú Falls (the most enormous volume of falling water in the world – double Niagara's), and the monumental statue of Christ the Redeemer who stood with outstretched arms on the highest mountain in Rio looking as if he were saying to all Brazilians, but particularly to the poor and under-privileged: 'I have given you the most beautiful country in the world; you are my people; I shall protect you'. All Brazilians believed it, not least the people of Cachoeira who, despite their isolation saw glimpses of glitz and glitter on black and white TV screens and a fair measure of military dictatorship propaganda. The poor, despite their grinding poverty, loved the shining glass buildings in which the rich lived and looked down on everything that had lost the glitter of novelty. The Edificio Oceania in Salvador, a handsome black-marble-clad art deco high-rise standing alone on a bluff overlooking the sea was despised because of its age. The words '*Ordem e Progresso*' or 'Order and Progress' (mischievously changed to '*Des-ordem e Retro-gresso*' by the ex-pat community) are written in bold letters on the national flag. Only progress is good, thought the poor, and only Third World countries such as Brazil can progress on a seismic and exciting scale: the Trans Amazonian Highway, to take an example, completed in 1972, is 5,300 kilometres long and links the Atlantic at João Pessoa (north of Salvador) with Peru. The road's steady progress was regularly followed in the news. No-one in those days paused to reflect on the possible long-term damage to the rain forest. Progress was all that mattered because with progress, as the TV programmes demonstrated, came wealth, and the thinnest layer of wealth to a country with as huge a population as Brazil's was a holy grail worth pursuing.

The Brazil we left in 1971 had the crazy ambition of a teenager with all the energy of youth standing on the threshold of a life full of boundless promise. The huge projects belonged to the moneyed classes who got richer at the expense of the poor. There was a time when inflation hit 100% and the hungry began to raid shops and supermarkets in search of food, but the high-rise buildings rose ever higher while the children of the upper classes flew to Europe and the United States for their education. One rich family from

Maceió had a large private jet which the children regularly commandeered to hop from one State to another while they bopped with their friends in the specially converted cabin. Such luxuries were in the same tradition as baskets of dirty laundry a few generations earlier making the round trip to Lisbon in search of clean water. It seemed to those who took a detached view of how Brazil was developing as a nation that in fact it wasn't developing at all. All the wealth remained with the rich who just got richer, while the spending power of tens of millions diminished. Anyone who spoke out was imprisoned and tortured, and those with a keener sense of self-preservation kept their thoughts very much to themselves, just like the Copacabana commuters in the Bank minibus after they had digested the alarming news that one of their fellow passengers had been removed during the night by the secret police.

In the late 60s and early 70s the plight of the poor was dire. When we went to say our last farewells to Carmen her eyes filled with tears, not so much on account of our imminent departure to a distant country across the sea, but because her resistance was at such a low ebb. Her real income now was much lower than before and she had lost all hope of being able adequately to feed her family. They all looked gaunt and lacking in nutrition. We knew a bit about that but we had untold riches to return to: a house that was the envy of our friends, long term deposit accounts, investments that had been gradually swelling in a stable economy, and the certain prospect of a good job. We might have eaten nothing but rice and beans for months but that was our choice. Carmen, Cécé and tens of millions like them were bent only on survival and their future looked bleak indeed.

No-one apart from the most far-sighted could have foreseen what has happened in the intervening years. President Lula, a one-time shoeshine boy who understood more than most what it means to have no hope, entirely transformed the country during his time in office. His successor, Dilma Rousseff, a guerrilla fighter from the seventies, imprisoned and tortured by the military dictatorship, stated in November 2010 that her ambition was to 'eradicate poverty'. Those of us who lived there forty years ago find it hard to consider this an attainable ambition although, apparently, she has every reason to be optimistic. The poor people with whom we lived had no vision of it: it was as if they had been born at the bottom of a deep ravine where the sun never shone and from which there was no deliverance. They were forced to accept their condition, and like subterranean beings never questioned what life could be like on the surface. Yoruba deities and the brothers of light maintained for them a link with a world where once or twice a week the poor could live on the same plane as them, experiencing for a short while what it was to have god-given powers and status in the community which they might not otherwise enjoy. But the rest of their lives was drab and uninspiring.

30

Brazil's living dead

We both came from traditions in England that viewed the souls of the departed as totally separate from the living, as if they were bricked up behind an impregnable wall, and any attempt to contact them (the ouija board, for example) was frowned upon. Even Arthur Conan Doyle, a Knight of the Realm and a man of recognised and considerable stature, was not immune when he became committed to Spiritism and risked destroying his stainless reputation in the gentlemen's clubs of Pall Mall. The modern western Christian tradition does not dabble with the spirits of the dead in any shape or form. 'Go forth, Christian soul, from this world' is what the Church of England says as the coffined body moves unsteadily out of the church towards the cemetery or crematorium. It is as if we were expelling the spirit from our midst. In Brazil, on the other hand, it is regularly welcomed back as a vital source of spiritual energy that heals.

During our year in the cult houses we had 'met' countless spirits, African, Amerindian and European, many good, a few bad, and witnessed their power to heal and comfort, and indeed we had noticed the similarities with some branches of Evangelical Christianity that claimed to heal 'with the power of the Holy Spirit'. But there was a subtle difference: the Christian tradition demands a belief in the power of the Holy Spirit, the third person of the Trinity. The Brazilian tradition expects more than that: certainly the Holy Trinity plays its part but not to the exclusion of other spirits and deities. On the contrary, it is the other spirits and deities which are to the fore, which 'control' the faithful and 'control' the plants and herbs which are used as part of the curing process. The Brazilian tradition is close to the jungle, the strange forces that are believed to reside in stones, plants, herbs and drums, all the forces that were rejected in England at the time of the Reformation which led to the decline of magic in the West. The Christian healing process today requires faith and adherence to religious dogma if the healing is to meet with any success. It rarely does.

In Brazil however, the long-standing tradition of trance and possession, the belief that evil dwells within and can only be expelled by forces of good, has resulted in African and Spiritist-based religions being at the very heart of healing, where sometimes the cult leader prepares the patient's body so that the multinational drug company's medicine will work. The prerequisite to success is that everyone, not simply the patient and the healer, has to believe in spiritual forces of good and evil. The belief can be channelled in various ways ranging from the ancient pantheon of African deities each of which has a rôle to play in the healing process, to the more recent Spiritism where enlightened spirits of the dead work through mediums and direct their healing 'energy' or 'currents' in such a way that the illness is arrested or cured outright.

The improbably named Dr Adolph Fritz, a German surgeon who died in a First World War field hospital in 1918, 'returned' in the 1960s to work with the first of the famous Spiritist healers, Zé Arigó. After Arigó's death he switched allegiance to another healer called, again very improbably, Oscar Wilde. He has since worked with Oscar's brother Edvaldo and various other healers and is currently with Rubens Farias, a healer with a huge following who opens up patients with a crude knife in order to remove whatever it is that is making them ill. The patients feel no pain and there are never problems with bleeding or infection. Other healers jab knives into eyeballs; one in particular has used an electric circular saw to cut through tissue and gain access to the part of the body in need of attention. Much of this has been well documented by professional observers and film crews. In a number of instances the healer himself has spent time with researchers in American universities. So far, however, nobody seems able adequately to explain how these healers can achieve such remarkable success rates, or how it is possible to take a circular saw to someone's back without him feeling any pain, then send him on his way a few minutes later. And yet these are remarkable daily occurrences in healing centres that operate free of charge from São Paulo in the south to Recife in the north. João de Deus (John of God) invites readers of his web page to click on a button if they wish to start a process of distant healing before arriving at his centre at Abadiania, a short distance from Brasília. *The Skeptics Dictionary (www.skepdic.com)* rejects much of this, questioning the validity of some of the claims. Of course there are instances of failure, but the many successes are there for everyone to see and we are still a long way from understanding how these mysterious forces can defy the rules that make it impossible for most people to plunge dirty knives in to eye sockets without inflicting any damage whatsoever. The healers say that they are the channel between this world and the world of the spirits, that it is in fact God, the *irmãos de luz* (brothers of light), the *correntes* (currents or energy forces), all acting together that heal the sick and make them whole.

Many will indeed want to dismiss this as so much bunkum, and it certainly appears to be bunkum to anyone brought up in the contemporary western tradition where nowadays the trance state is mainly induced by hypnotists to entertain mass audiences at University Graduation Balls or on television. But when you witness it working for the common good of a broad cross-section of Brazilian society you cannot but believe that there are forces, still not properly understood, that can and do work for the good of all. Moreover, these so-called primitive practices and beliefs are so firmly entrenched in Brazilian society that they will easily survive whilst the economy grows into one of the biggest in the world.

International drugs companies should note that Brazilian-style African and Spiritist-based healing has a well proven track record and that cult priests and priestesses have an intimate knowledge of the healing properties of hundreds of different plants. Drugs companies would do well to familiarise themselves with what is already common knowledge in cult houses throughout the country in the hope that some of the herbal lore might at some stage in the future be developed in the laboratory and made available to a wider public. We should hope that the Brazilian government in the meantime will need no reminding that these healing processes constitute an invaluable resource that, with proper support, could provide a network of care that could easily dovetail in to a modern national health system. The economic and social advantages of such a scheme would be considerable: ancient beliefs and modern medicine working together, the one supporting the other.

Lorca's famous utterance '...a dead person in Spain is more alive when dead than is the case anywhere else...' would be clearly understood in Brazil where an accomplished man's skills, developed and honed over a life time, need not simply disappear when his body ceases to breathe. Those he left behind can continue to benefit from his knowledge and experience particularly if, when alive, he practised as a doctor or a surgeon. The man we met in Salvador went every Thursday to lay hands on cancer patients in the guise of a local and much admired surgeon who had died some years before. Quietly and without a fanfare of trumpets he arrested the onward creep of the disease. The rational part of my being does not permit me to dismiss this remarkable fact.

Acknowledgements

I owe a very considerable debt to Shell who forty years ago were the only international company with South American connections who responded favourably to our begging letter, offered to transport us to Brazil to undertake fieldwork, and then twelve months later delivered us safely back to Britain. We were students at the time with very limited resources and our whole project would have been seriously jeopardised if someone in Shell had not responded to our request for help. The only condition was, quite understandably, that we should mention Shell as sponsors if any of our work were published. We duly did this in 1978 on the publication of *Primitive Religion and Healing: A Study of Folk Medicine in Brazil* and I am more than happy to do so again now. Warm thanks too to Simon Woolley for drawing the maps and to Matthew and Marjorie Huntley who brought all their experience and expertise to the reading of the first draft. My wife Rosie, the best of editors, has excelled, as ever, in scrutinising the text, picking me up on details and making apposite suggestions. This project which enabled us to focus on our various and remarkable experiences in Brazil forty years ago has made us realise how much we owe to the many people of Bahia who willingly shared their secrets with us and welcomed us so warmly in to their homes. They may never see this book but their contribution has been immeasurable.